# Small State Referendum

This book explores the unusual and unique experience of direct democracy in the small state of New Zealand, where referendums have been a persistent feature of the political landscape for over a century. Referendums have been the site of renewed interest from scholars, seeking to respond to what they term the "democratic deficit" in otherwise stable and functional Western democracies. They have also been at the heart of many divisive and important political and social moments in recent history, from the UK's Brexit referendum in 2016 to the disputed legitimacy of the 2022 referendums in Russian-occupied Ukraine. This book fills an important gap in the literature through an extended study of the law and practice of referendums in the small Commonwealth state of New Zealand. It also expands the field of small state democracy studies by applying the insights of this field to the direct democracy experience of a small state. With the inclusion of comprehensive tables of referendums and legislative materials, this book will be of interest to scholars of direct democracy and small states, politicians, legislators and policy makers, and all those with a desire to do democracy better.

**Caroline Morris** is Reader in Public Law at Queen Mary University of London, UK.

# Small State Referendums
Lessons from New Zealand

**Caroline Morris**

Routledge
Taylor & Francis Group

LONDON AND NEW YORK

First published 2025
by Routledge
4 Park Square, Milton Park, Abingdon, Oxon OX14 4RN

and by Routledge
605 Third Avenue, New York, NY 10158

*Routledge is an imprint of the Taylor & Francis Group, an informa business*

© 2025 Caroline Morris

*British Library Cataloguing-in-Publication Data*
A catalogue record for this book is available from the British Library

*Library of Congress Cataloging-in-Publication Data*
Names: Morris, Caroline, 1973- author.
Title: Small state referendums : lessons from New Zealand /
Caroline Morris.
Description: Abingdon, Oxon [UK]; New York, NY:
Routledge, 2024. | Includes bibliographical references
and index.
Identifiers: LCCN 2024015463 (print) | LCCN 2024015464
(ebook) | ISBN 9781032741956 (hardback) | ISBN
9781032760414 (paperback) | ISBN 9781003472452 (ebook)
Subjects: LCSH: People (Constitutional law)–New Zealand. |
Referendum–New Zealand. | Representative government and
representation–New Zealand. | Election law–New Zealand. |
Proportional representation–New Zealand. | Political
participation–New Zealand. | New Zealand–Politics and
government. | Referendum.
Classification: LCC KUQ2174 .M67 2024 (print) | LCC
KUQ2174 (ebook) | DDC 328.2/30993–dc23/eng/20240409
LC record available at https://lccn.loc.gov/2024015463
LC ebook record available at https://lccn.loc.gov/2024015464

ISBN: 978-1-032-74195-6 (hbk)
ISBN: 978-1-032-76041-4 (pbk)
ISBN: 978-1-003-47245-2 (ebk)

DOI: 10.4324/9781003472452

Typeset in Times New Roman
by Deanta Global Publishing Services, Chennai, India

For Richard, Charles, and Frederick

# Contents

# Preface

This book, and my interest in referendums, had their beginnings nearly a quarter of a century ago on the 13th floor of the Charles Fergusson building in Wellington, New Zealand. As a new public servant in the Ministry of Justice I was asked over morning tea one day what I thought of the rather long and multi-faceted referendum question on criminal justice that would be asked at the upcoming 1999 general election. This casual question led me not to an answer, but to many more questions in return. It contained multiple topics and was confusing—what was meant by terms such as "restitution and compensation," "hard labour," or a "serious violent offence"? It could be said to have contradictory ends—was it punitive or focused on victims of crime? How did you vote if you supported some of the elements of the question but not others? What was the use of such a question? How would the government respond if the people voted in favour? Was this uncertainty the fault of the Citizens Initiated Referenda Act under which it was being held, or the political system in which it was taking place? I soon departed the public service for academia but my interest in referendums has remained. This book is part of the journey into the different forms of direct democracy and their legal framework that I have been on ever since.

As always, no book is truly a solo endeavour. I would like to thank my friend and fellow adventurer in the world of referendums, Professor Matt Qvortrup, for suggesting that I write on this topic. I would like to thank the editorial team at Routledge, Colin Perrin, Alison Kirk, and Anna Gallagher for welcoming my initial proposal, supporting it through the review and approval processes, answering my questions, and keeping me to deadline as I finished the manuscript. Thank you also to the anonymous reviewers whose helpful comments encouraged me, sharpened my thinking, and led me in new directions. Special thanks are due to Katharine Kilroy who provided exemplary research assistance, made light work of all of my formatting idiosyncrasies, accommodated my last-minute requests for changes, and was unfailingly cheerful throughout. I am particularly indebted to her for her work on referendums in small states and for compiling the tables of referendums contained in the Appendices.

Every effort has been taken to ensure that the material in this book is up to date as of 31 January 2024. All errors and omissions remaining are my responsibility.

Dr Caroline Morris
Queen Mary University of London
London

# Table of Legislation

# 1 Introducing referendums and the small state

## Introduction

This book tells the story of a small state, namely New Zealand, and its experience of the referendum. It is not a work of grand theory on direct democracy. Others have written those books (see Tierney, 2012). Nor is it an exercise in quantitative or empirical analysis of the referendum experience (see Altman, 2010). And it is not a comparative overview of constitutional and political practice relating to this particular form of democracy, such as those written by Butler and Ranney (1994) or Qvortrup (2018). In this book, I also put to one side the questions of whether referendums are good or bad per se and whether the people have the capacity for voting on the questions put to them. What this book offers is something different. It seeks to paint a picture of a particular democratic experience and place it within a particular frame.

First, it offers a deeper exploration than can be found in the existing direct democracy literature of New Zealand history and experimentation with different forms of the referendum. Though often identified as a curious, adventurous, or atypical case of direct democracy, New Zealand has rarely been afforded more than a paragraph or two in the mainstream and generally Euro- or American-centric literature. Its experience is not generally treated as important or exemplary, unlike Switzerland or the states of the US. As Elkins and Hudson (2022, p.45) observe, studies of direct democracy tend to focus on "the usual suspects" and this does not include New Zealand.

In this book, I trace the history of New Zealand's referendum experience from the last decade of the 19th century through the first two and a half decades of the 21st, starting with the triennial referendums on alcohol licencing that lasted nearly a century, to the sporadic and at times seemingly unsystematic referendums on questions of social and constitutional importance, and the adoption of citizen-initiated referendums in the last decade of the 20th century. In the course of covering this wide variety in the content and form of referendums in New Zealand, I consider three key aspects of this history: the origins and underlying rationales for referendums, the factors influencing the outcome of a referendum, and the political and legal consequences of referendums. This exploration reveals a creative approach to the use of direct

DOI: 10.4324/9781003472452-1

democracy, far from the "second-best" alternative to representative democracy that often bedevils the characterisation of referendums. This book also contains details of referendums and the accompanying legislation that have not been brought together before, even in New Zealand. It will therefore act as a resource for scholars of referendums, curious politicians, and law drafters who will be able to examine the approach taken to legislating for referendums in the absence of a written constitution specifying how referendums should be held, and see how this has changed over time and in response to increasingly complex matters.

Second, this book tackles the issue of direct democracy from a little-studied angle: that of the small state. Small states are known to be more "democratic" than their larger counterparts. However, studies of democracy in small states have tended to focus on representative democracy and the existence of civil liberties and human rights observance and protection (see Corbett and Veenendaal, 2018). Of less prominence is the examination of the small state experience of direct democracy (with the exception of Anckar, 2004 and 2020). It is not clear whether small states are more likely to incorporate direct democracy into their political practice. Altman (2011, p.78) considers the impact of population negligible, although he also observes that "the more democratic a regime is, the more likely it is to use [direct democracy measures]" (Altman, 2010, p.81) which is salient to the status of small states as democracies (on which see below). More recently, Bruggemann et al.'s (2023, p.8, fig. 2.3) research reveals that, of the top ten users of referendums, six are small states: New Zealand, Liechtenstein, the Northern Mariana Islands, the Federated States of Micronesia, the Marshall Islands, and Palau. In addition, since New Zealand comes second only to Switzerland in the number of referendums held worldwide since 1900 (Bruggemann et al., 2023, p.8, fig. 2.3), this provides us with an excellent opportunity to explore how a small state deploys the referendum within its wider democratic system.

Third, almost all analyses of direct democracy are undertaken with an emphasis on the *political* context. This is unsurprising, for a referendum is the example par excellence of democratic politics. Yet referendums are mandated or enabled by *law* and conducted under particular legal rules, any or all of which may influence the experience and the result, even the possibility of a referendum being held in the first place. As a common law constitutional lawyer (for a civil law/soft law analysis see Moeckli, Forgács and Ibi, 2021), I bring the role of law in the referendum to the foreground and take a relational view of how these two key levers of state power—law and politics—influence each other in the practice of the referendum. That is, what is the role of law in the creation and conduct of the referendum, and how has the referendum been used by politicians and the public to "do" politics through law outside the sphere of representative democracy?

In addition to these three points of difference, this book adds a new voice to the increasing attention being paid to referendums across the world (e.g. Matsusaka, 2020; Smith, 2021; Albert and Stacey, 2022). As disillusionment and disengagement with representative politics become more obvious, not only through traditional markers of engagement such as voter turnout and membership of political parties (Corbett and Veenendaal, 2018, pp.92–93), but also through acts of violent insurrection, such as the storming of the US Capitol on 6 January 2021 under the belief that the 2020 US presidential election had been rigged, referendums are sometimes seen as a corrective to failures of representative democracy, restoring the citizen voice in the forum of public affairs and enhancing popular sovereignty over an out-of-touch or elitist government (Conti, 2023, pp.xxxii–xxxiii). The goal is not always to win the vote or determine the view of the people on a particular question, but to engage the people in the democratic process, granting authenticity to the outcome and agency to the participants (Linder and Mueller, 2021, p.139). Others see direct democracy as a supplement to its representative counterpart, supplying an additional level of legitimacy to the decisions of elected representatives (Butler and Ranney, 1994, pp.13–14). Others still note that referendums can be used to give the veneer of democracy to decisions promoted by non-democratic regimes (Albert and Stacey, 2022, p.16–17).

In 2022, Albert and Stacey (2022, p.32) declared "we are in the midst of the age of the referendum. And that age will not soon end." The past two decades have seen more referendums than ever conducted (Tierney, 2012, p.11), many of them high-profile: in 2013, the people of the Falkland Islands chose to remain under British rather than Argentinian control; in 2015, the voters of Ireland endorsed changing the Irish Constitution to permit same-sex marriage; Britain's "Brexit" referendum on European Union membership in 2016 (Atkinson, Blick and Qvortrup, 2020); in 2016, the people of Thailand voted to approve a draft constitution put forward by a military junta; in 2018, Bolivians rejected an amendment to the Constitution that would have permitted the-then President to serve a fourth term; in the same year, the people of Bougainville voted almost unanimously for independence from Papua New Guinea while a referendum in New Caledonia in 2021 saw the option of independence from France overwhelmingly rejected; the disputed legitimacy of the 2022 annexation referendums in Russian-occupied Ukraine, and most recently, Australia's failed referendum on the establishment of an Aboriginal and Torres Strait Islander advisory body to the Australian federal Parliament and Government in October 2023.

## The small state

In focussing on the small state experience of referendums, the immediate question that must be answered is: what do we mean when we speak of the "small state"?

The most common determinant for a small state is population size. Organisations such as the Commonwealth Secretariat and the World Bank define a small state as one with a population of 1.5 million people or less (Thorhallsson, 2018, p.18). Other bodies, such as the UN Forum of Small States, established by Singapore and currently led by New Zealand, set the bar at 10 million people or less. Others, such as Corbett and Veenendaal (2018) have employed 1 million people as the determinant of small. Yet even these bright-line rules can be bent: some states may exceed the population criteria but nonetheless exhibit many of the features and face the same challenges as states which come within the population rule. For this reason, we see that the Commonwealth Secretariat includes both Jamaica (popn. 2.83 million) and Papua New Guinea (popn. 11.78 million) within the class of small states, and the World Bank includes an additional 10 states to the 40 which meet the population requirements for its Small States Forum. Population measures are sometimes used together with the size of a state's economy (gross domestic product) and/or its territory. Sometimes states with small populations also have small economies and small territories. However, this is not always the case. A state with little territory may have a large population, economy, and military capability; and so be powerful. On the other hand, states with extensive territory can also have small economies.

Another measurement takes into account of political matters. These include: the ability of small states to maintain sovereignty over their territory and govern it efficiently and capably; the military and administrative power of the state, the ability of the state to form a foreign policy consensus, and the domestic cohesion needed to tackle various problems (Baldacchino and Wivers, 2020, p.7). This factor is linked back to population—states with low populations can struggle to defend themselves from aggressors, staff their government and civil service, and represent themselves on the world stage.

These are objective measures. An alternative is to consider a state's "perceptual size." Perceptual size is determined by the political discourse surrounding a state (self-generated or otherwise) and the views that leaders, elites, civil society groups, and the public have of their own states. Small states that perceive themselves as influential actors with a role to play in world politics may be more successful in making a mark, whereas small states that do not believe that they can ever be influential on the world stage end up victims of this self-fulfilling prophecy. Perceptions by outside actors of the state in question are also relevant.

Relational size is another way of assessing whether a state is small. To a European state such as San Marino, with a population of 34,000, claims to smallness by states such as Sweden or Norway might seem questionable. But when compared to their close neighbours Russia, France, and Germany, Sweden and Norway may well consider themselves small based on many factors, including population, territory, and power. A similar situation arises in the Pacific. To the many microstates of the Pacific, New Zealand is a large power with ample territory, a developed economy, a transparent and functional government, and a population of five million people. But in the New Zealand psyche, when it considers its Pacific Rim counterparts Australia, Japan, the US, Canada, and Mexico, it is simply not in the same category. Both in relational and perceptual terms, New Zealand considers itself a small state.

## Why study the small state?

Many of the world's states are small states. They comprise around 20% of the UN's member states and also the majority of the Commonwealth's 56 states. Despite these numbers they are still overlooked as a legitimate site of study. But as Neumann and Gstöhl (2006, p.3) tell us, "small states are simply too numerous and – sometimes individually, but certainly collectively – too important to ignore."

Veenendaal and Corbett (2015) make a strong case for the study of small states. One reason the study of small states is a worthwhile endeavour, they argue, is that all states, no matter their size, can contribute insights and new understandings. If they share features with larger states, then why not include them in our dataset? If they are different—small states often exhibit somewhat "unusual political and legal institutions" (Wolf et al., 2018, p.185)—then this too is valuable. While some describe these differences as "deviant" (Veenendaal and Wolf, 2016, p.279) in that they do not always fit an orthodox or expected template, these distinctive institutions and systems provide an opportunity to study a particular form of government, institutional design, or new ways of making law. If we study those states we have not previously included, then surely we can add more to the sum of our knowledge than by simply studying those we are already familiar with (Veenendaal and Corbett, 2015, p.530). To exclude small states from our inquiries runs the risk of weakening our scholarship and undermining our conclusions. In relation to New Zealand, it has long had a reputation as a social and political innovator. It was an early creator of the welfare state, and has engaged in radical reform of several areas of law, from personal injury litigation to the electoral system. Most recently, New Zealand was hailed worldwide for its decisive and effective approach to the Covid-19 pandemic. In this book, I explore an understudied aspect of this distinctive phenomenon through an assessment of the New Zealand approach to direct democracy.

## Democracy in a small state

Over 50 years ago, the US political scientists Robert Dahl and Edward Tufte idealised the small state as the paradigm of the democratic experience (Dahl and Tufte, 1973). This idea was enthusiastically pursued by several researchers who determined, using the classic indicators of democracy, that small states were more likely to be "democratic" than their larger counterparts (Diamond and Tsalik, 1999; Srebrnik, 2004). Small states that were also islands were even more likely to be assessed as democracies (see Anckar, C. and Anckar, D., 1995; Anckar, C., 2008; Ott, 2000).[1] Typical indicia included a government elected by popular vote, by free, fair, and regular elections with a universal franchise, the upholding of civil liberties and human rights, a commitment to the rule of law, an absence of military rule, an independent legislature and judiciary, a system of responsible and accountable government (including an effective opposition and room for dissent), and measures for transparency of government, particularly in relation to public funds.[2] We can also include a system of checks and balances, including a separation of powers that enables effective government while avoiding conflicts of interest, a free and independent press, and a non-authoritarian political culture.

More recently, the scholars Jack Corbett and Wouter Veenendaal (2018) presented an alternative perspective on small state democracy (see also Veenendaal, 2015a; 2015b). Focussing not on the formal markers of democracy but on the underlying experience of democracy, they identified a core, overarching characteristic of small state democracy, that of "hyper-personalisation" (Corbett and Veenendaal, 2018, pp.9–10). Hyper-personalised small state politics sees the public sphere take on a more expansive societal role than in larger ones; and in that public sphere, not only are the links between politicians and the public close and unmediated, individuals (political or otherwise) can have a disproportionate impact on that public life (Corbett and Veenendaal, 2018, pp.172–178). Many of the referendums that have taken place in New Zealand illustrate these claims.

### A typology of referendums

Those seeking to understand the referendum will soon find themselves enmeshed in a great variety of definitions and attempts to explain the role that various direct democracy devices play in a polity. What follows is a brief overview of the most common ways in which the referendum has been categorised.

---

1 Very few of the world's small states are not islands, and those that are not are clustered in Europe (Andorra, Monaco, Luxembourg, Liechtenstein, San Marino, and the Vatican). Some of these are nonetheless considered "islands" by virtue of their being enclosed by larger states, just as other states are surrounded by the sea.
2 Freedom House, the international monitoring organisation and the only one of its type to include small states within its dataset, assesses states for their commitment to "democratic political environments where governments are accountable to their own people; the rule of law prevails; and freedoms of expression, association, and belief, as well as respect for the rights of minorities and women, are guaranteed." See www.freedomhouse.org.

One approach is to classify referendums according to their subject-matter (Altman, 2010, p.209). These tend to fall into two groups. The first is what we might term the self-determination referendum, posing the critical question of independence or secession from another state or, occasionally, a multinational grouping such as the European Union or the North Atlantic Treaty Organization (NATO) (see Tierney, 2013a, pp.2191–2192; Altman, 2010, p.310). The second is a catch-all grouping for popular votes on questions of high political or moral significance for which popular endorsement is seen as imperative (Altman, 2010, p.310). Into this grouping would fall issues such as electoral reform, same-sex marriage, and drug decriminalisation. This group can also include another angle of analysis, that is, whether the question itself can be seen as reactive or proactive. The former is the classic understanding of the referendum—a public vote on whether an enacted law should come into force—as practised in Switzerland (see Linder and Mueller, 2021) and repeatedly championed by Dicey as a practice Britain should adopt (Conti, 2023).

Another approach is to look at the originator of the referendum (Altman, 2010, p.211). This can be "from above" if it comes from the government, legislature, or is required by a provision of a state's constitution, or "from below" when the call for a referendum is initiated by the people (Linder and Mueller, 2021, pp.120–126).

A third approach is to categorise the referendum by its resultant effect (Altman, 2010, p.211): will the vote be binding or simply advisory?

In addition to these lenses, a further typology classifies referendums according to their stages: will the electorate be asked a single question, once, or multiple questions successive times? Yet another classification is the binary referendum where the voter has a choice of two options versus the multi-option referendum (Wagenaar and Hendriks, 2021, pp.372–373).

Yet another layer of analysis can be added to any one of these types of referendum through a consideration of the rules surrounding the process of the referendum. For example, there may be restrictions on who may vote (Adam, Kagiaros and Tierney, 2018, pp.265–272) or what may be the subject of a referendum; special rules and processes may apply to determining the wording of a referendum question; voting may be compulsory or optional; legitimacy thresholds may apply to the turnout or the result or both (such as the double majority rules that apply to changes to the Australian Constitution (Williams and Hume, 2010)); the outcome and/or the processes may be justiciable or not (on which see Miller, 2009; Moeckli, Forgács and Ibi, 2021); voting in a referendum may take place solely in person, only by post, or a combination; and there may be spending limits on campaigns surrounding the referendum (see Qvortrup, 2021, pp.93–138). Each of these in turn adds a level of complexity to our understanding of the referendum. In combination, and when looking at the categories of subject matter, origins and effect, we can see that the appropriate model for referendum design and/or analysis looks not like a spectrum or table but something more akin to a spider's web.

## Conclusion

This book seeks to bring together the study of two previously unconnected areas of public life: the small state and the referendum. Small states are well-known for being democracies; referendums are considered the ideal type of democratic practice. Although it is not clear whether small states consistently make use of referendums more than larger states, the small state of New Zealand has been a frequent deployer of referendums throughout its history, holding single question referendums and multi-option, multi-stage referendums, binding referendums and advisory referendums, repeated questions and singular questions. In the following chapters, this experience is explored in depth to add to the sum of knowledge on small state democracies and to see what we might learn from it.

## References

Adam, E.C., Kagiaros, D. and Tierney, S. (2018). 'Democracy in Questions? Direct Democracy in the European Union', *European Constitutional Law Review*, 14, pp.261–282.

Albert, R. and Stacey, R. (eds) (2022). *The Limits and Legitimacy of Referendums.* Oxford: Oxford University Press.

Altman, R. (2010). *Direct Democracy Worldwide.* Cambridge: Cambridge University Press.

Anckar, C. and Anckar, D. (1995). 'Size, Insularity and Democracy', *Scandinavian Political Studies*, 18(4), pp.211–229.

Anckar, C. (2008). 'Size, Islandness and Democracy: A Global Comparison', *International Political Science Review*, 29(4), pp.433–436.

Anckar, D. (2004). 'Direct Democracy in Microstates and Small Island States', *World Development*, 32(2), pp.379–390.

Anckar, D. (2020). 'Small States: Politics and Policies', In Baldacchino, G. and Wivers, A. (eds). *Handbook on the Politics of Small States.* Cheltenham: Edward Elgar. pp.38–54.

Atkinson, L., Blick, A. and Qvortrup, M. (2020). *The Referendum in Britain: A History.* Oxford: Oxford University Press.

Baldacchino, G. and Wivers, A. (2020). 'Small States: Concepts And Theories', In Baldacchino, G. and Wivers, A. (eds). *Handbook on the Politics of Small States.* Cheltenham: Edward Elgar. pp2–19.

Butler, D. and Ranney, A. (eds) (1994). *Referendums Around the World.* Basingstoke: Palgrave Macmillan.

Brüggemann, S., Gut, R., Serdült, U. and Wüthrich, J. (2023). *The World of Referendums: 2023 edition.* Zurich: Centre for Democracy Studies Aarau.

Conti, G. (ed) (2023). *Albert Venn Dicey Writings on Democracy and the Referendum.* Cambridge: Cambridge University Press.

Corbett, J. and Veenendaal, W.P. (2018). *Democracy in Small States: Persisting Against All Odds.* Oxford: Oxford University Press.

Dahl, R.A. and Tufte, E.R. (1973). *Size and Democracy.* Redwood City: Stanford University Press.

Diamond, L.J. and Tsalik, S. (1999). 'Size and Democracy: The Case for Decentralization', in Diamond, L.J. (ed). *Developing Democracy: Towards Consolidation*. Baltimore: Johns Hopkins University Press. pp.117–160.

Elkins, Z. and Alexander, H. (2022) 'The Strange Case of the Package Deal: Amendments and Replacements in Constitutional Reform', in Albert, R. and Stacey, R. (eds). *The Limits and Legitimacy of Referendums*. Oxford: Oxford University Press. pp.37–62.

Linder, L. and Mueller, S. (2021). *Swiss Democracy*. Berlin: Springer.

Matsusaka, J. G. (2020). *Let the People Rule: How Direct Democracy can meet the Populist Challenge*. Princeton: Princeton University Press.

Miller, K.P. (2009). *Direct Democracy and the Courts*. Cambridge: Cambridge University Press.

Moeckli, D., Forgács, A. and Ibi, H. (eds) (2021). *The Legal Limits of Direct Democracy: A Comparative Analysis of Referendums and Initiatives Across Europe*. Cheltenham: Edward Elgar.

Neumann, I.B. and Gstöhl, S. (2006). 'Introduction: Lilliputians in Gulliver's world?', In C. Ingebritsen et al. (eds). *Small States in International Relations*. Seattle, WA: University of Washington Press. pp.3–36.

Ott, D. (2000). *Small is Democratic*. New York: Garland.

Qvortrup, M. (ed) (2018). *Referendums Around the World – The Continued Growth of Direct Democracy*. 2nd edn. Berlin: Springer.

Qvortrup, M. (2021). *Democracy on Demand: Holding Power to Account*. Manchester: Manchester University Press.

Smith, J. (ed) (2021). *The Palgrave Handbook of European Referendums*. Cham: Palgrave Macmillan.

Srebrnik, H. (2004). 'Small Island Nations and Democratic Values', *World Development*, 32(2), pp.329–341.

Tierney, S. (2012). *Constitutional Referendums: The Theory and Practice of Republican Deliberation*. Oxford: Oxford University Press.

Tierney, S. (2013a). 'Whose Political Constitution?', *German Law Journal,* 14(12), pp.2185–2196.

Thorhallsson, B. (2018). 'Studying Small States: A Review', *Small States and Territories,* 1(1), pp.17–34.

Veenendaal, W.P., and Corbett, J. (2015). 'Why Small States Offer Important Answers to Large Questions', *Comparative Political Studies*, 48(4), pp.527–549.

Veenendaal, W. and Wolf, S. (2016). 'Concluding Remarks: Achievements, Challenges, and Opportunities of Small State Research', In Wolf, S. (ed). *State Size Matters: Politik und Recht im Kontext von Kleinstaatlichkeit und Monarchie*. Berlin: Springer. pp.277–284.

Veenendaal, W.P. (2015a). 'Democracy in Microstates; Why Smallness Does Not Produce a Democratic System', *Democratization*, 22(1), pp.92–112.

Veenendaal, W.P. (2015b). *Politics and Democracy in Microstates*. London: Routledge.

Wagenaar, C. C. L. and Hendriks, F. (2021). 'Setting the Voting Agenda for Multi-option Referendums: Process Variations and Civic Empowerment', *Democratization*, 28(2), pp.372–393

Williams, G. and Hume, D. (2010). *People Power: The History and Future of the Referendum in Australia*. Sydney: UNSW Press.

Wolf, S., Bussjager, P. and Schiess Rutimann, P.M. (2018). 'Law, Small State Theory and the Case of Liechtenstein', *Small States and Territories*, 1(2), pp.183–196.

# 2 The New Zealand experience of the referendum

## Introduction

New Zealand is a country known for both its social and constitutional innovation. Since its establishment as a modern state in 1840, New Zealanders have
experienced a wide variety of "firsts" and unique moments in the fields of
social and constitutional development.

In 1893, New Zealand became the first country to grant women the right to
vote. It is also regarded as having established one of the first comprehensive
social welfare systems in the developed world. A system of old-age pensions
was introduced in 1898 by the Liberal government (public servants had had
their own scheme since 1894), followed by a widows' pension in 1910, and a
system of state acquisition of land for workers' housing was created in 1905,
as well as many other reforms in the areas of workers' rights, access to education, women's rights, child welfare, and public health. Particular attention
was paid to improving the position of the indigenous Māori people, who had
suffered extensively from the impacts of colonisation.

Representative government was established in New Zealand in 1852 and
the country has been a stable democracy with free and fair elections ever
since. In 1962, New Zealand was the first country outside of the Nordic
states to implement the position of an Ombudsman to investigate government
wrongs and provide the public with a remedy. In 1972, all personal injury
suits were outlawed[1] and replaced with a state-run no-fault accident compensation scheme. In the early 1990s, it also reformed its electoral system, aban-
doning its British-inherited First-Past-the-Post (FPTP) system in favour of the
German-style Mixed Member Proportional (MMP) system. In the same time
period, legislation providing for nationwide citizen-initiated referendums was
enacted, again, an unusual democratic choice for a Commonwealth country,
and the first of which to do so.

Referendums are an established part of the New Zealand constitutional
fabric, having been used at both a national and local level from the early

---

1 This had been the case for workers since 1900 under the Workers' Compensation Act.

DOI: 10.4324/9781003472452-2

stages of government. The first local referendum took place in 1894 and the first national referendum in 1911. In contrast, New Zealand's colonial power, Great Britain, did not hold its first sub-national referendum until 1973 (on Northern Ireland's potential reunification with Ireland) and its first nationwide referendum until 1975 (on membership of the then European Economic Community). The referendums that have been held in New Zealand reflect the two areas of reform identified above, being clustered around the poles of social and constitutional change: alcohol licencing, gambling, drug reform, and assisted dying at one end, and electoral, parliamentary, and sovereignty issues at the other. In this chapter, I explore the history of these referendums, first placing them in their constitutional and political context, and then considering the various factors that led to their being held and their impact on New Zealand law and political practice.

## Provisions for referendums

The reasons why countries adopt direct democracy measures as part of their constitutional arrangements tend to be country-specific and the product of a particular political and/or social movement. This is certainly the case for New Zealand, in both the case of government-led and citizen-initiated referendums. Where New Zealand deviates from typical practice is that all referendums are governed by ordinary legislation and in most cases, specific legislation is enacted to govern the particular referendum. This places direct democracy in a more vulnerable position than its representative counterpart. It also means that comparisons between government-led referendums are less straightforward, as each referendum has its own unique catalyst, and may have particular rules about status, campaign spending, and the method of balloting.

## The origins of referendum provisions in New Zealand

Much academic work addressing national referendums begins by assuming that the constitution is the first and most significant place to look for provisions relating to referendums (Bogdanor, 1994, pp.25–30). In New Zealand, such an approach would be futile, for New Zealand has no single document supreme law text known as "the Constitution". Instead, the New Zealand constitution very much resembles its British counterpart and is comprised of ordinary law statutes, the common law, and practices and conventions governing the exercise of political power. Parliament, not the judiciary, wields ultimate constitutional and legal power. Also significant is the Treaty of Waitangi, the 1840 instrument of cession of sovereignty from the Māori people to the British Crown.

There is therefore no systematic or overarching guidance determining why, how, and when a referendum might be held. No topics are deemed to be off-limits or indeed required to be the subject of a referendum (save for the term of Parliament and a few provisions relating to elections).[2] Instead, referendums are enabled either through specific enabling legislation for government-initiated referendums or under the Citizens Initiated Referenda Act 1993 (CIR Act) for those initiated by the people. This follows a classic pattern of referendum typology, employed by many scholars of referendums, including Walker (2003, p.9), Altman (2010, p.2), Qvortrup (2018b) and Hollander (2019, p.43).

Referendums first became a part of the political scene in New Zealand via the Alcoholic Liquors Sale Control Act 1893. The Act brought together the personal temperance-sympathetic politics of Liberal Party Premiers Robert Stout and his successor Richard Seddon, with the underlying political philosophy of the governing Liberal Party that "conformity of government policy to the wishes of the 'democracy' had been declared to be the basis of Liberal politics since 1890" (Hamer, 1988, p.117). This philosophy was evident in the New Zealand legislature generally, as the House of Representatives (the elected lower chamber) had in 1893 resolved that the people "should have the power to settle, by direct vote, the question of [liquor] licenses" (House of Representatives 1893, vol. 80, p.379). These views were also reflected in the Long Title of the Act which was "An Act to Give the People Greater Control over the Granting and Refusing of Licenses."[3] This move to direct democracy on the alcohol vote also aligned with the common practice, sourced in deep party divisions on the matter, of treating alcohol sales not as a matter of party politics but for the conscience of the individual legislator (Lindsey, 2008).

This legislation provided for local referendums on the sale of alcohol within a particular district. Residents could choose for their area to be "wet" or "dry". This approach was expanded with the Licensing Amendment Act 1910, which provided for national referendums on the question of alcohol sales, including an option for prohibition. While neither Premier Seddon nor his successor Joseph Ward were prohibitionists, pressure from temperance groups and the liquor trade associations since the 1893 Act (Christoffel, 2008, pp.156) led both leaders to seek a compromise that avoided their having to make a decision one way or the other on what has been described as "one of the most politically divisive issues of New Zealand's early decades" (NZ Law Commission, 2009, p.21).

In 1911, the first nationwide referendum took place under the Licensing Act. Referendums were subsequently held every three years at the same time as the general election, save for postponements relating to World Wars I and II and the Great Depression (see generally Prince, 1996). The final alcohol

---

2  Electoral Act 1993 (NZ), s 268. Even then a referendum may be avoided if a super-majority of 75% of the Parliament is in favour of amendment or repeal.
3  Although "licence" is the term ordinarily used in UK and NZ English, the use of the US spelling "license" appears to have been employed throughout in this context.

sales referendum took place in 1987 when, following a review of alcohol sales and availability legislation in 1986 (Laking, 1986), the government decided that the long-standing preference for the status quo coupled with the declining vote and influence of the Prohibition movement justified discontinuing the practice of licencing referendums.[4] The Sale of Liquor Act 1989 abolished the triennial alcohol referendums, liberalised the sale of wine and beer outside of licenced premises, and set the scene for other reforms such as a reduction of the legal drinking age.

Outside of the alcohol sales referendums, referendums did not feature as a means of determining the will of the people until 1949. These stand-alone referendums were intermittent, with 19 taking place in the past 73 years. This seeming degree of caution in their use is also seen in their status. Referendums in New Zealand are almost always advisory. In the case of the five CIR Act referendums, their non-binding nature is provided for in the governing legislation. This leaves government-initiated referendums, of which there have been 14 outside of the triennial liquor poll. Of these, only three have been binding: the 1993 electoral reform vote and the 2020 end of life and cannabis reform referendums. Interestingly, in these cases, legislation had already been enacted by the Parliament with a provision that it would come into force following its endorsement at the referendum. All were also preceded by long-running campaigns, both within parliament and in civil society, which kept the issue in the public domain and allowed for extensive debate of the issues. The binding nature of the 2020 referendum was secured as part of the price of minor party support for cannabis reform legislation, and the binding 1993 vote was promised by both major political parties at the time.

## New Zealand's referendums types and history

New Zealand has experience of both types of "originator" referendums: government-initiated since 1911, and citizen-initiated from 1993. Both of these types have addressed the different categories of subject matter referendums, with constitutional and policy referendums alike featuring in its political history. Multi-stage referendums have become increasingly popular with the government, and multi-option referendums have been used in New Zealand since the early days of referendum use. In this next section, I classify and then sketch out the different referendums that have been held between 1949 and 2022 and provide some background on their genesis.

---

4 It is nonetheless worth noting that after dropping from 40.2% in 1928 to 29.6% in 1935, the Prohibition vote remained relatively stable and still registered 20.7% at the final referendum in 1987 (see Appendix II).

## Government-initiated referendums

*Single-option referendums*

The most common form of referendum globally is the single-issue vote. New Zealand has had a small number of these but the timing has been sporadic. One year will see two (1967 and 2020) or even three (1949) referendums, with long gaps of around 20 years in between these bursts of direct democracy activity. All of these referendums have fallen into either the social or constitutional categories.

The first use of a typical referendum occurred in 1949, a scheduled general election year. After 14 years in power, the Labour Party was riven by internal differences and losing its public appeal. The government, not wishing to alienate its support base further, or find itself on the wrong side of divisive social issues, decided to put difficult questions directly to the public (Jackson, 1973, pp.61–62). Two referendums on social issues took place in March 1949, one on gambling reform (allowing off-course betting), and the other on the extension of pub opening hours beyond 6pm. The latter question also conforms to the New Zealand legislature's practice of deferring to the public will on matters relating to alcohol consumption (seen again in 1967). New Zealanders voted to relax their gambling laws but to keep their pubs closed in the evenings. A further referendum was held in November 1949 on the subject of compulsory military training. This latter referendum was the result of a bargain between the opposition National Party, which had this as a policy goal, and the ruling Labour Party. National supported the earlier two referendums in return for Labour supporting a third (Jackson, 1987, p.29). This was approved and a system of compulsory military training for young men was put in place from 1950 to 1972.

After this flurry of referendums, nearly two decades passed. On 23 September 1967 a double referendum was held. One asked whether the term of parliament should be extended from three to four years (Royal Commission on the Electoral System, 1986, p.156). The other revisited the question of whether pubs should be allowed to be open past 6pm. This time, New Zealanders endorsed longer drinking hours but said no to a longer parliamentary term. Jackson (1987, p.29) has commented that this twinning was a strategic choice: the government wished to relax licencing laws and so brought in what it knew would be an unpopular proposition so that New Zealanders could have "something to vote against while easing licensing hours."

Another two decades passed before the next single-option referendum was held. The question of the term of parliament was put to the people again at a referendum held at the same time as the general election on 27 October 1990. Again, New Zealanders said no to extending the term to four years. Another single-issue referendum was held in 1997. This was the first referendum conducted by postal ballot over a three week period (5–26 September 1997). New

Zealanders decisively rejected the proposal that there should be a compulsory retirement savings scheme with 91.8% voting against it.

A further two decades again passed before New Zealand reverted to the double referendum for the third time. On 17 October 2020, New Zealanders were asked to vote in two separate referendums, one on the decriminalisation, and regulation of recreational cannabis, and the other on assisted dying. In a repeat of the vote split seen in the earlier two double referendums of 1949 and 1967, the cannabis reforms were rejected while the assisted dying regime was approved.

*Multi-option referendums*

As noted, New Zealand's extensive and unique experience with referendums properly began in 1911. In that year, the first of what would become a triennial event was held: this was the nationwide liquor poll, which asked New Zealanders whether they wished to adopt prohibition or continue with the existing system of alcohol licencing and sale (termed "national continuance"). In 1918, a third option was added, that of state control of the industry. The prohibition of alcohol was a movement of considerable global impact and New Zealand was no exception (Dostie and Dupré, 2016, pp.491–493). Perhaps because so much progressive social reform had already been achieved by the long-ruling Liberal government (1891–1912), the temperance movement was able to occupy a societal and political space that in other nations was more crowded.

The vote in 1911 was in favour of prohibition and would have seen New Zealand become the first country in the world to adopt prohibition, save for the 60% in favour threshold imposed by the legislation (Dostie and Dupré, 2016, p.492). Prohibition had been endorsed by "only" 55.8% of the voters, and so was not introduced. Prohibition continued to be a popular cause in New Zealand, winning large proportions of the vote in subsequent referendums although never again coming close to its early successes (Dostie and Dupré, 2016, pp.501–502). The polls were finally discontinued in 1987 but by then multi-option referendums were firmly embedded as a New Zealand political practice.

Multi-option referendums were chosen again for two referendums that went to the heart of New Zealand's political and cultural life. As observed by Qvortrup (2018a, p.60), referendums are often criticised for reducing complex questions to a simple binary choice, casting doubt as to the integrity of the question and the reliability of the response. Although rare, multi-option referendums, in contrast, are said to empower citizens with greater choice, reduce conflict by blurring the faultlines of disagreement, and encourage creativity in the policy options to be voted on (Wagenaar and Hendriks, 2020, p.373). As Tierney (2013) notes, New Zealand's use of what has been termed the "gateway, filter and run-off" model over two referendums has been successful in achieving these goals (see also Bogdanor, in Tierney, 2013, p.9)

The first referendum of this type was a referendum on whether New Zealand should change its voting system, and if so, to what alternative system. This referendum in 1992 was the eventual outcome of a review of the electoral system commissioned by the government in 1986. A long period of authoritarian government combined with two "wrong winner" elections in 1979 and 1982 had left New Zealanders distrustful of and disappointed in their democracy. In an unexpected turn, the Royal Commission on the Electoral System (RCES) recommended the adoption of the German MMP system, along with other reforms such as extending the term of parliament (RCES, 1986, p.295–302). A large majority of the public responded in Part A that they wished to change the electoral system from FPTP and in Part B, a smaller majority nominated MMP as the system that should replace FPTP. A second, single-issue referendum was held the following year asking New Zealanders to choose between MMP and FPTP in which MMP emerged the winner. The first election under the new system was held in 1996, ushering in an era of coalition and minority governments (the first majority government under MMP was elected in 2020) and markedly changing the composition of the legislature from one dominated by two parties alternating in government to a multi-party, multi-government body. Membership of the legislature was also transformed, with significant increases in the representation of women, Māori, other ethnic minorities (notably Pasifika and Asian) and other members from under-represented groups, such as the disabled and transgender communities.

In 2011, this two-stage referendum was revisited, but this time the staging was reversed. New Zealanders were first asked whether MMP rather than FPTP should be retained. The second question asked voters which of four alternative systems they would prefer, with the most popular to be selected for a run-off against MMP the following year should the public vote for change. As MMP received 56.2% of the vote at the first stage, the second referendum did not take place.

The most recent multi-option referendum took place over several months between November 2015 and March 2016. This concerned whether New Zealand should reflect its changing national identity in a change of flag. In the first referendum, held by post from 20 November–11 December 2015, voters were asked if the flag were to be changed, which of five options would they prefer. The second postal vote referendum took place between 3 and 24 March 2016 where the current flag was pitted against the preferred design from the earlier vote. New Zealanders voted to retain the existing flag by 56.6%.

### Citizen-initiated referendums

Direct democracy measures in the New Zealand political landscape were added to with the enactment of the Citizens Initiated Referenda Act in 1993.

The procedure required for a referendum to be held requires firstly, the submission of a potential petition and the prescribed fee to the Clerk of the House of Representatives. Upon approval of the wording, the petitioner has 12 months to collect the required number of signatures, that is, 10% of those on the electoral roll (approximately 350,000 people). If the threshold is met, then a referendum must be held. If not, the petition lapses. These requirements are not easy to meet, and so far, only five referendums have been held under the CIR Act. The record reveals that after an initial flurry of activity, recourse to petitions has slowed considerably. In addition, there are now long gaps between petitions. The last decade has seen six CIR potential petition questions of the total of 52 submitted since the first in 1994, when 18 questions were submitted. Two were submitted in 2018, one on methods of wild pest control and the other on the creation of a new city, one was submitted in 2020 on the decriminalisation of cannabis, one in March 2022 on the preservation of Māori custom and one in January 2023 on whether "adequate housing" should be a legally enforceable right (all since lapsed). There is only one petition currently at the signature collecting stage. Promoted by a local council, it asks "should the New Zealand government fund road maintenance at levels sufficient to reverse the current decline in the average age and condition of our national state highway network?"

The five referendums under the CIR Act defy neat subject matter categorisation. The first was held on 2 December 1995 as a standalone vote. Sponsored by the New Zealand Professional Firefighters Union in response to a government restructuring exercise, it asked whether the number of professional firefighters should be reduced. While the public overwhelmingly sided with the Firefighters' Union, the very low turnout of 28% casts doubt on the robustness of the response and lessened the political impetus to respond (Wehrle, 1997, p.289).

Two CIR Act referendums took place at the same time as the general election on 27 November 1999. One asked a very simple objective question. The other asked a rather complex subjective question with multiple elements. To the question "Should the size of the House of Representatives be reduced from 120 members to 99 members?" 81.5% of voters said "yes." The other question, "Should there be a reform of our Justice system placing greater emphasis on the needs of victims, providing restitution and compensation for them and imposing minimum sentences and hard labour for all serious violent offences?" was even more enthusiastically endorsed, with 91.8% voting "yes."

A decade passed before a petition was able to meet the threshold for another CIR Act referendum to be held. This was in response to legislation perceived as unpopular in certain sections of the community. The repeal of a Crimes Act defence to an assault charge based on reasonable chastisement of a child in 2007 was controversial. A lobby group called Focus on the Family joined forces with a dissatisfied MP to hold a CIR Act referendum asking "should a smack as part of good parental correction be a criminal offence in New Zealand?" The vote was conducted by post over three weeks between 31 July and 21 August 2009. A resounding 87.4% responded "no."

The most recent CIR Act referendum occurred in 2013. This was a challenge to the government's proposed programme of partial privatisation of four energy state-owned enterprises and the national air carrier, Air New Zealand. The Asset sales (Mixed Ownership Model) referendum was also conducted by postal vote, taking place between 22 November and 13 December 2013. Two-thirds of those voting (67.3%) cast their ballot against the government's privatisation plans.

## Local referendums

Local referendums were the first type of referendum employed in New Zealand. As noted, it was the Alcoholic Liquors Sale Control Act 1893 which introduced the referendum to New Zealand politics in a systematic manner. This Act allowed voters to decide whether their local district should be "wet" or "dry" through a binding vote that would see the closure of all bars and liquor sales outlets in the area.[5] A majority of 60% was required for this to take effect. Notwithstanding the supermajority rule, by 1908, Christoffel (2008, p.156) noted that 484 hotel bars had been closed as a result of the "local option" vote, and 12 out of 76 electorates had voted to abolish liquor sales. These local referendums continued throughout the 20th century until the last four "dry" local districts voted to become "wet."

Local referendums outside the context of liquor sales appear to have been first enabled by the Local Elections Act 1904 (subsequently re-enacted and consolidated several times as the Local Elections and Polls Act 1908–1966). This legislation enabled local authorities to hold a poll on any proposal they thought fit. It also set out the rules for local referendums required under certain legislation such as the changing of the basis on which local rates were charged or the raising of a special loan outside the authority's usual remit. Use of this mechanism was sporadic and, while multiple polls on the system of rates based on land valuation were held in the early part of the 20th century across multiple districts in New Zealand (including 25 between 1910 and 1913 alone (1913 Yearbook)), Bush noted that, by the mid-1990s, they were a "relatively rare phenomenon" (Bush, 1995, p.291). Nevertheless, the 1990s did still see nine local referendums on whether a local authority should obtain a specific loan.

---

5 A precursor to this Act was the Licensing Act 1881 which provided that no new alcohol licences could be issued within a particular area without the holding of a local poll (which could only be held triennially and was not binding).

In the modern era, the Local Electoral Act 2001 provides the foundation for local referendums. A local authority may direct a referendum be held on current or future services provided by local authority or matters which are directly within its remit of activity. Various referendums have been held under these provisions, ranging from fluoridation of local water supplies (of which there have been dozens), investment in a local museum and the amalgamation of regional authorities. The referendum provisions were also used on a number of occasions to overturn local authority decisions to establish "Māori wards" (particular representation for the Māori people on the same basis as the reserved seats for Māori in the national legislature). In response, the Labour government then in power oversaw the enactment of the Local Electoral (Māori Ward and Māori Constituencies) Amendment Act 2021, which removed the ability to use local referendum procedures to challenge provision for dedicated Māori representation. The right-leaning government that was elected following the October 2023 election has signalled its intent to restore the ability to hold referendums on local Māori representation.

## Reasons for referendums

### *The "democratic deficit"*

Much writing on referendums assumes a binary approach to democratic practice, with a choice to be made between the direct and representative forms. The surge in the use of referendums is explained as a reaction to the failures of representative democracy (Hollander, 2019, pp.9–11; Mendelsohn and Parkin, 2001, p.1). Resort to direct democracy replaces the power of the "corrupt elite" with that of the "pure people" (Greaves et al., 2021, p.134). Was this also the case with New Zealand?

At first glance, the enactment of the Citizens Initiated Referenda Act in 1993 certainly fits this pattern. Previous attempts to introduce citizen-initiated referendum legislation in New Zealand had all failed (Morris, 2004, p.120). But in the two decades preceding the CIR Act, the New Zealand public experienced significant dissatisfaction with traditional forms of representative democracy.

Once the era of three-party politics had transitioned to a two-party system by the 1930s, Aimer observes that this had proved to be an "extraordinarily robust" model (1989, p.261) for nearly half a century. However, by the 1970s, New Zealand had begun to experience the phenomena of partisan and class dealignment as well as greater electoral volatility (Aimer, 1989, pp.263–270; Vowles, 1995, pp.102–103). This was not the outcome of gradual decline but could be specifically traced to "three consecutive extraordinary elections—1978, 1981, 1984" (Aimer, 1989, p.264).

In 1975, the National Party won the election and Robert Muldoon became the Prime Minister, a position he was to hold until 1984. Muldoon "was frequently criticised for being excessively confrontational and divisive" (Mulgan, 1989, p.454) and his government oversaw an era in New Zealand politics noted for excessive regulation, government by diktat, and disregard for the niceties of the law. Criticism was not limited to one politician or party however. On the style of New Zealand politics prevalent in those two decades, Palmer (1987, pp.254–255) wrote "we have a combative adversary style of politics … we tend to descend to personalities quickly and offensively … balance, moderation, care with the facts and fair-mindedness are not attitudes encouraged by our existing system."

Immediately before the 1993 election, James and McRobie wrote (1993, pp.1–2):

> For nine years [under the Labour government 1984–1990 and National 1990–1993] a programme of economic restructuring has been followed for which Cabinet had no popular mandate and limited subsequent popular support … most have received little personal benefit from … and some no benefit at all …. relative economic decline has been accompanied by diminishing personal security as the number of crimes against property and the person has risen … Many New Zealanders feel that government by the two major parties during the past twenty years has amounted to a massive breach of promise—of specific promises, implied and inferred promises and the overarching promise imputed to all New Zealand governments that they should not leave the country worse than they found it.

The impact of these experiences was made clear by public opinion polls, with McRobie (1994, p.103) noting that, according to a long-standing question asked by the Heylen Research Centre, New Zealanders' level of trust and confidence in politicians had declined from 32% in 1975 to 4% in 1992. In the same year, the *National Business Review* Respect List ranked politicians 19th out of 21 occupations, above only insurance representatives and car dealers.

The "political disaffection" hypothesis proposes that as people become more disconnected and alienated from traditional representative democracy, referendums provide an opportunity for re-connecting with politics, to voice their thoughts on particular issues, and to feel heard (Greaves et al., 2021, p.134). In response to what they saw as New Zealand's increasingly autocratic and illiberal governance under the Muldoon administration, the two-member Social Credit Party attempted to place direct democracy measures on the policy agenda by introducing a Popular Initiatives Bill into the New Zealand Parliament in 1984 (Mapp, 1995, p.446). The Bill did not proceed but was referred to the Royal Commission on the Electoral System for their consideration.

However, in response to growing political alienation in New Zealand, the Royal Commission recommended electoral reform over referendums, terming them "blunt and crude devices" (RCES, 1986, p.175). This proposal was not popular with politicians. As well as challenging MMP and championing FPTP, the ruling National Party in particular put effort into alternatives to electoral reform in the hope that this might dampen the appeal of MMP. One of these was the re-establishment of a legislative upper chamber, which had been abolished in New Zealand in 1951 (Renwick, 2007, pp.14–16), and the other was what was to become the Citizens Initiated Referenda Act. The former proposal was quickly dropped but the idea of direct democracy became very popular within certain sections of the National Party (Church, 2000, p.186). Parkinson (2001, pp.407–408) notes that this sector of the National Party came under pressure from two civil society groups to adopt direct democracy in response to what they saw as government dismissal of the opinions of the New Zealand people. These two groups were the Coalition of Concerned Citizens, formed in the wake of 1986 legislation decriminalising male homosexuality and banning discrimination on the basis of sexual orientation, and the One New Foundation, which was opposed to government moves in the mid-1980s to provide redress for long-standing Māori grievances.

In short, citizen-initiated referendums in New Zealand were implemented primarily as a device for diverting popular dissatisfaction with politicians into a proposed tool of (re)empowerment, and thereby, to forestall the prospect of long-term and systematic electoral reform. This movement was complemented by the pressures placed on a sympathetic faction within the governing party with two pro-referendum alliances.

### Legitimacy

A further justification for referendums is that some issues cannot legitimately be decided by the people's representatives but need to be determined by the people themselves (Walker, 2003, pp.4–5). This also features in the New Zealand experience. "Conscience" issues, such as alcohol and cannabis consumption, gambling, and end of life decisions were all handed over to the people to decide on via a public vote.

Similarly, Renwick (2007, p.20) identifies three senior National Party politicians as being instrumental in the decision to promise the referendums on electoral reform. Despite any personal misgivings they might have had about MMP, they felt it was the right thing to do to let the people decide the question.

### Personalised politics

New Zealand is a relatively small country in global terms, with a population of 5 million. Politics can be very personalised in such states (Corbett and Veenendaal, 2018, pp.176–178) with individual politicians having disproportionately large profiles and influence on public debate. Two very senior politicians, the then Prime Minister John Key and the then Deputy Prime Minister

Winston Peters, were able to control the political process to the extent that government-led referendums were held on their pet issues (a change of flag and compulsory retirement saving respectively), despite the lack of public interest in these topics generally (Trevett, 2015).

At the other end of political practice, in small nations, private individuals can also become players on the political stage in a way that might not be possible in larger countries. This phenomenon can be seen in the clear identification of three referendums with particular individuals and their own personal interest or stake in the topic: Margaret Robertson on parliamentary reform, Norm Withers on criminal justice reform, and Lecretia Seales on assisted dying. Each of these became the public face of the referendum debate, despite having no public persona or history of political activism previously.

Robertson was a self-described "battling Karori [a large Wellington suburb] grandmother" who claimed she was motivated to launch her campaign after listening to Parliament on the radio: the unexpected formation of a coalition government, and the antics of an influx of new MPs involving "underpants and drunken pugilistics" had not impressed Robertson (Church, 2000, p.189). Withers was a Christchurch shopkeeper whose mother was brutally assaulted by an individual with 56 prior convictions while she was working in her son's shop (Church, 2000, p.192). Seales was a young Wellington lawyer who conducted a very public struggle, including litigation, to gain autonomy over the end of her life following a diagnosis of terminal brain cancer (Vickers, 2016). This personal investment in the issue in particular was instrumental in bringing the issue to the attention of the wider New Zealand public as well as the success of the passing of the End of Life Choice Act where the legislature had not been able to agree to pass similar laws in the past.

### Referendums as political strategy

The use of referendums does not appear to be the preserve of any particular party. Only one party, New Zealand First (NZ First), and in particular its leader, Winston Peters, has expressed a preference for decision-making via referendums, but it has itself been instrumental in the holding of only one. Occasionally, political parties have been formed on a direct democracy platform, but they appear to have limited appeal to the New Zealand electorate and are short-lived.

#### Government-initiated referendums

Mendelsohn and Parkin (2001, p.8) observe that referendums can be used as a tool for managing conflict between the parties to a coalition. New Zealand has not experienced this phenomenon; rather, on at least two occasions, a government-initiated referendum on a particular issue was the price extracted from a majority party for the support of a minority party. This development could not have occurred before the change to MMP in 1996, which resulted in majority coalition governments or minority governments supported through confidence and supply agreements between 1996 and 2020.[6] The surety for governance was paid by both major parties, the centre-right National Party in 1996, and the centre-left Labour party in 2017. Two very different minor parties employed this tactic. The socially conservative populist NZ First party secured a referendum on a compulsory national retirement savings scheme (known as "superannuation" in New Zealand) in 1997[7] and the social democratic Green party obtained one on cannabis law reform in 2020.[8]

As befits their origins, both referendums were the subject of extensive political shaping before the question was put to the public. In the superannuation referendum, the key elements of the scheme were set out in a coalition agreement. These were worked up by public servants who also referred to the superannuation policy of NZ First (Preston, 1997, pp.145–146). A government White Paper was issued in July 1997 (Preston, 1997, p.146) and the final specifics of the scheme were set out in the Compulsory Retirement Savings Scheme Referendum Act 1997. Clause 19 of the Labour-Greens agreement stipulated that there should be a "referendum on legalising the personal use of cannabis at, or by, the 2020 general election." Although the reforms were put in more general terms, the details were prepared by public servants following the government's decision to prepare draft legislation which the public could approve or not (Little, 2019). Following its introduction to the legislature, the Cannabis Legalisation and Control Bill was referred to a cross-party parliamentary committee which received evidence from experts and members of the public alike.

The November 2023 general election resulted in a right-leaning coalition between the larger National Party and the smaller Association of Consumers and Taxpayers (ACT) and NZ First parties. Perhaps inspired by these earlier examples, part of the price of securing the support of the ACT party was a commitment to introduce legislation which would define the principles of the Treaty of Waitangi and make provision for a binding referendum to confirm or reject the law. However, on 23 January 2024, the Prime Minister distanced himself from the referendum plans, following significant backlash from the Māori community spearheaded by the Māori King (head of the influential Kiingitanga movement) (McKay, 2024).

6  In 2020, the Labour party became the first party to form a government on its own since the introduction of MMP.
7  NZ First party coalition agreement with the National Party 9 December 1996.
8  Green party coalition agreement with Labour Party 24 October 2017.

*Citizen-initiated referendums*

Political parties have also employed the Citizens Initiated Referenda Act to advance their policy position on at least three occasions. Curiously, this has not been a tactic of the NZ First party, which has been the only party to publicly advocate for greater use of referendums.

Following the rejection of the proposed reforms in the Cannabis Legalisation and Control Bill, a member of the youth wing of the Green party (Young Greens) launched a CIR petition advocating a more modest change to cannabis laws, focussing on decriminalisation rather than a full suite of legalisation of use and commercial regulation. Asking "Should it remain a criminal offence to possess cannabis for personal use?", the petition failed to have gathered the required number of signatures by the deadline of 22 February 2022. It was then declared to have lapsed by the Clerk of the House of Representatives (*NZ Gazette*, 2022, p.755).

A similar response was seen in the actions of the Kiwi Party 15 years previously. In May 2007, the Parliament amended a section of the Crimes Act by removing the provision that had permitted parents to use "reasonable force" for the purposes of disciplining children. The minority United Future party was in favour of the change. In response, Larry Baldock and Gordon Copeland left United Future to form the Kiwi Party (initially known as the Future party). Larry Baldock was the co-sponsor of the successful petition to hold the referendum querying the amendment.

The Greens and the Labour party also co-operated in sponsoring the referendum on national asset sales. Although nominally headed by the President of Grey Power, the campaign was in the hands of the Keep Our Assets pressure group, which was dominated by the Green and Labour parties (Dawson and Andriopoulos, 2017, p.145). In an unprecedented cross-over between representative and direct democracy, the Green Party was discovered to have used its parliamentary funds to hire eight staff to collect petition signatures (NZ Herald, 2012).

A recent interesting development in the use of the CIR Act was its deployment by a local authority to press the government to improve national road conditions. In 2023, the New Plymouth council submitted the following question to the Clerk of the House of Representatives for approval: "Should the New Zealand government fund road maintenance at levels sufficient to reverse the current decline in the average age and condition of our national state highway network?" The Mayor of the council justified the use of the CIR process by referencing his struggles to attract funding for road maintenance from the central government and concluded by saying "this initiative reflects that what I thought was a local issue, is actually a national issue" (Coster, 2023). At the time of writing, signatures are being collected in support of holding a referendum on this question.

*Accidental referendums*

In other cases, the decision to hold a referendum has been much less calculated. It has become part of New Zealand political lore that the 1992 referendum on electoral reform only took place because the then Prime Minister David Lange misread his speech notes at a televised leaders' debate in 1987, and committed his party to holding such a referendum should they be re-elected (Jackson, 1993, p.18). The Labour party was re-elected but the referendum did not take place. At the campaign for the next election in 1990 the Opposition National Party attempted to make political capital of this broken promise and made a promise of their own to hold a binding referendum on electoral reform (Renwick, 2007, pp.8–9). National duly won the election and was obliged to keep its promise.

The most recent referendum on the electoral system also had less than august origins. There was a widespread misconception amongst the New Zealand public that the adoption of MMP was not necessarily permanent, but to be revisited at some point in the future. This had its roots in an article in the *Listener* radio and television listings magazine prior to the 1993 referendum which stated that there was nothing to lose by voting for MMP because voters would have the chance to return to FPTP in 2002 (Jackson and McRobie, 1998, p.199). The view was not accurate, but it had great persistence. Not even the scheduled review of MMP by a parliamentary committee in 2001 alleviated the calls for another referendum. Indeed, Arseneau and Roberts (2012, p.326) note that the committee's failure to recommend that another referendum on MMP only intensified the expectation that one ought to be held. In response, the National Party made it a manifesto promise in 2008 to hold such a referendum. Upon winning that election, the referendum was held in 2011. MMP received even greater endorsement in 2011 than it had in 1993.

## Conclusion

New Zealand was an early adopter of the referendum as part of its political machinery. To some extent, the use of the referendum followed the classic justification that certain matters ought to be decided directly by the people rather than their representatives. National referendums on alcohol licencing rules were held every three years from 1911 and others on topics of social or constitutional concern were held sporadically in clusters from 1949. However, the early 1990s saw an explosion in the use of the referendum. This reflected not only the attempted constitutional reforms (some successful, some not) and resulting political developments of the decade but also the introduction of legislation in 1993 permitting individuals to petition for a referendum on virtually any topic of their choosing. A similar pattern can be seen in the experience of local referendums which were first legislated for in 1904. Both types of referendums have a clear link to the increasing political disaffection and growing mistrust of politicians experienced by New Zealanders from the 1978 election onwards: to address this, the people were asked whether they wished to change their voting system while at the same time they were to be given another outlet for the expression of their views outside the ballot box.

In addition, the New Zealand experience reveals that the referendum can transcend its initial purpose or role in the political system. Following the shift to coalition government under the MMP system endorsed by the referendum in 1993, political parties have on three occasions (1997, 2020, and 2023) sought to have the holding of a referendum made part of the coalition or support agreement. Parties have used the Citizens Initiated Referenda Act in the same way (albeit less successfully), being behind CIR Act referendums challenging child chastisement laws and asset sales policies. As well as these uses of the referendum as a strategic device, it is well known in New Zealand that the momentous referendums of 1992 and 1993 which led to the change in the electoral system to MMP originated from some misread speech notes, and the 2011 referendum on MMP's retention had its roots in a throw-away comment in a national television listings magazine. Particular individuals have also been critical of the adoption of the referendum: from the temperance sympathies of Premiers Robert Stout and Richard Seddon that led to the alcohol licencing referendums to the personal struggles of the terminally-ill Lecretia Seales that eventually resulted in the referendum that endorsed the End of Life Choice Act 2019.

## References

Aimer, P. (1989). 'The Changing Party System', In Gold, H. (ed). *New Zealand Politics in -Perspective.* 2nd edn. Auckland: Longman Paul. pp.260–274.

Altman, D. (2010). *Direct Democracy Worldwide.* Cambridge: Cambridge University Press.

Arseneau, T. and Roberts, N. (2012). '"Kicking the Tyres on MMP": The Results of the Referendum Reviewed', In Johansson, J. and Levine, S. (eds). *Kicking the Tyres – The New Zealand General Election and Electoral Referendum of 2011.* Wellington: Victoria University Press. pp.325–346.

Bogdanor, V. (1994). 'Western Europe', In Butler, D. and Ranney, A. (eds). *Referendums Around the World.* Basingstoke: Palgrave Macmillan. pp.24–97.

Bush, G. (1995). *Local Government & Politics in New Zealand.* 2nd edn. Auckland: Auckland University Press.

Christoffel, P. (2008). 'Prohibition and the Myth of 1919', *New Zealand Journal of History,* 42(2), pp.154–175.

Church, S. (2000). 'Crime and Punishment: The Referenda to Reform the Criminal Justice System and Reduce the Size of Parliament', In Boston, J., Church, S., Levine, S. and McLeay, E. (eds). *Left Turn: The New Zealand General Election of 1999.* Wellington: Victoria University Press. pp184–199.

Corbett, J. and Veenendaal, W.P. (2018). *Democracy in Small States: Persisting Against all Odds.* Oxford: Oxford University Press.

Coster, D. (2023). 'New Plymouth Council pushing for Nationwide Petition On Road Funding', *Taranaki Daily News*, 25 May. Available at: https://www.stuff.co.nz/taranaki-daily-news/132123146/new-plymouth-council-pushing-for-nationwide-petition-on-road-funding (Accessed: 24 January 2024).

Dawson, P. and Andriopoulos, C. (2017). *Managing Change, Creativity & Innovation*. 3rd edn. London: Sage.

Dostie, B. and Dupré, R. (2016). 'Serial Referendums on Alcohol Prohibition: A New Zealand Invention', *Social Science History*, 40(3), pp.491–521.

Greaves, L.M., Oldfield, L.D. and Milne, B.J. (2021). 'Let the People Decide? Support for Referenda since the New Zealand Flag Change Referendums', *Kōtuitui: New Zealand Journal of Social Sciences Online*, 16(1), pp.1–15.

Hamer, D.A. (1988). *The New Zealand Liberals*. Auckland: Oxford University Press.

Hollander, S. (2019). *The Politics of Referendum Use in European Democracies*. London: Palgrave Macmillan.

House of Representatives Deb. (1893). vol.80. Available at: https://hdl.handle.net/2027/uc1.32106019787735 (Accessed: 22 January 2024).

Jackson, K. (1973). *New Zealand: Politics of Change*. Wellington: Reed Education.

Jackson, K. (1987). *The Dilemma of Parliament*. Wellington: Allen and Unwin.

Jackson, W.K. (1993). 'The Origins of the Electoral Referendums', In McRobie et al. (eds). *Taking it to the People*. Christchurch: Hazard Press. pp.15–23.

Jackson, K. and McRobie, A. (1998). *New Zealand Adopts Proportional Representation*. Christchurch: Hazard Press.

James, C. and McRobie, A. (1993). *Turning Point: The 1983 Election and Beyond*. Wellington: Bridget Williams Books.

Laking, G. (1986). *Report of the Working Party on Liquor: The Sale of Liquor in New Zealand*. Wellington: NZ Government.

Lindsey, D. (2008). 'A Brief History of Conscience Voting in New Zealand', *Australasian Parliamentary Review*, 23, pp.144–171.

Little, A. and Minister of Justice. (2019). *Cannabis Referendum – Legislative Process and Overarching Policy Settings for the Regulatory Model*. Wellington: Cabinet Paper.

Mapp, W. (1995). 'New Zealand's System of Citizens Initiated Referenda', *Agenda: A Journal of Policy Analysis and Reform*, 2(4), pp.445–454.

McKay, B. (2024). 'NZ PM Luxon Rules Out Treaty of Waitangi Referendum', *The Examiner*, 23 January. Available at: https://www.examiner.com.au/story/8496154/nz-pm-luxon-rules-out-treaty-of-waitangi-referendum/ (Accessed: 24 January 2024).

McRobie, A. (1994). 'Final and Binding: The 1993 Electoral Referendum', In Vowles, J. and Aimer, P. (eds). *Double Decision*. Wellington: Department of Politics, Victoria University of Wellington. pp.101–124.

Mendelsohn, M. and Parkin, A. (eds) (2001). *Referendum Democracy*. Basingstoke: Palgrave Macmillan.

Morris, C. (2004). 'Improving Our Democracy or a Fraud on the Community? A Closer Look at New Zealand's Citizens Initiated Referenda Act 1993', *Statute Law Review*, 25(2), pp.116–135.

Mulgan, R. (1989). 'New Zealand – An Elective Dictatorship?', In Gold, H. (ed). *New Zealand Politics in Perspective*. 2nd edn. Auckland: Longman Paul. pp.446–456.

NZ Gazette. (2022). *Notice that Indicative Referendum Petition has Lapsed*. Wellington. 4 March. Available at: https://gazette.govt.nz/assets/pdf-cache/2022/2022-ps755.pdf?2022-03-11_07%3A41%3A28= (Accessed: 22 January 2024).

NZ Herald. (2012). 'Greens use of Public Cash for Petition Wrong', *NZ Herald*, 21 July. Available at: https://www.nzherald.co.nz/nz/editorial-greens-use-of-public-cash-for-petition-wrong/PG25HTGYN5LH2GGZ6U2UEVMXOQ/?c_id=1&objectid=10814355 (Accessed: 22 January 2024).

NZ Law Commission. (2009). *Review of Regulatory Framework for the Sale and Supply of Liquor Part 1: Alcohol Legislation and the Conscience Vote.* Wellington: NZLC.

Palmer, G. (1987). *Unbridled Power.* 2nd edn. Auckland: Oxford University Press.

Parkinson, J. (2001). 'Who Knows Best? The Creation of the Citizen-initiated Referendum in New Zealand', *Government and Opposition*, 36(3), pp.403–422.

Preston, D.A. (1997). 'The Compulsory Retirement Savings Scheme Referendum of 1997', *Social Policy Journal of New Zealand*, 16(1), pp.138–150.

Prince, J.L. (1996). 'Look Back in Amber: The General Licensing Poll in New Zealand, 1919-87', *Political Science*, 48(1), pp.48–72.

Renwick, A. (2007). 'Why Did National Promise a Referendum On Electoral Reform in 1990?', *Political Science*, 59(1), pp.7–22.

Royal Commission on the Electoral System. (1986). *Report of the Royal Commission on the Electoral System: Towards a Better Democracy.* Available at: https://web.archive.org/web/20170524153410/http://www.elections.org.nz/voting-system/mmp-voting-system/report-royal-commission-electoral-system-1986 (Accessed: 22 January 2024).

Tierney, S. (2013). 'The Multi-option Referendum: International Guidelines, International Practice and Practical Issues'. University of Edinburgh Research Paper Series. 2013/33.

Trevett, C. (2015). 'Flag Show at Half Mast', *NZ Herald*, 17 July. Available at: https://www.nzherald.co.nz/nz/flag-show-at-half-mast/2WZJ3TYQAILVKQPTK27DJHCMC4/?c_id=1500876&objectid=11482801 (Accessed: 22 January 2024).

Qvortrup, M. (2018a). 'Mob Rule or the Wisdom of the Crowds: Reflections on Referendums and Public Policy', *Brown Journal of World Affairs*, XXIV(2), pp.57–69.

Qvortrup, M. (2018b). *Direct Democracy: A Comparative Study of the Theory and Practice of Government by the People.* 2nd edn. Manchester: Manchester University Press.

Vickers, M. (2016). *Lecretia's Choice: A Story of Love, Death and the Law.* Wellington: Text Publishing.

Vowles, J. (1995). 'The Politics of Electoral Reform in New Zealand', *International Political Science Review*, 16(1), pp.95–115.

Wagenaar, C.C.L. and Hendriks, F. (2020). 'Setting the Voting Agenda for Multi-option Referendums: Process Variations and Civic Empowerment', *Democratization*, 28(2), pp.372–393.

Walker, M. (2003). *The Strategic Use Of Referendums: Power, Legitimacy, And Democracy.* New York: Palgrave Macmillan.

Wehrle, G. (1997). 'The Firefighters' Referendum - Should Questions Arising from Industrial Disputes be excluded from a Referenda held under the Citizens Initiated Referenda Act 1993?', *Victoria University of Wellington Law Review*, 27(2), pp.273–299.

# 3    Referendums in context

## The timing of referendums

Referendum scholars typically propose that the timing of referendums can be linked to institutional factors and political expediency. Certain features of the political party system, particularly struggles between elites (Walker, 2003, p.17), are also sometimes posited as relevant. In New Zealand's case, it would seem that the former is more of a factor in the timing of a referendum, along with levels of public engagement in the issues, rather than inter- or intra-party bargaining (although this is also sometimes relevant) or limitations on legislative capabilities (Walker, 2003, p.11).

New Zealand's Parliament is one of the few worldwide that has no substantive limitations on its ability to legislate. Referendums are therefore not needed to compensate for any deficit in legislative capacity. New Zealand also has the distinction of having one of the world's shortest parliamentary terms. Elections are held every three years for a single chamber. This increases the opportunity (and the likelihood) that referendums will be held at the same time as a general election. This is indeed the case. The vast majority of referendums in New Zealand have been held alongside a general election, both for logistical reasons and in the hope of increasing turnout (see Appendices). Previously infrequently held, with only five referendums outside the liquor polls being held between 1949 and 1989, the 1990s saw a remarkable increase in the use of referendums in New Zealand politics. Seven referendums were held in nine years.

Turnout was clearly affected when the referendum was not held at the same time as a general election. The notable exception was the 1997 compulsory superannuation referendum, which was conducted by postal vote. In that referendum, turnout was sustained at levels close to that of a parliamentary election. The impact of turnout on the legitimacy of the result as well as the cost implications of a standalone referendum led to the enactment of the Referenda (Postal Voting) Act 2000. This provides for the holding of an indicative referendum (government initiated or under the CIR Act) by postal vote over a three-week period. But as Table 3.2 shows, postal voting on its own has not restored turnout to levels seen at a referendum held at a general election.

DOI: 10.4324/9781003472452-3

*Table 3.1* Referendums held between 1990–1999

| Year | Subject | Type | Turnout |
|---|---|---|---|
| 1990 | Term of Parliament | Government | 85.2% * |
| 1992 | Electoral Reform I | Government | 55.2% |
| 1993 | Electoral Reform II | Government | 85.2% * |
| 1994 | Firefighters' numbers | CIR | 27.0% |
| 1997 | Superannuation | Government | 80.3% |
| 1999 | Number of MPs | CIR | 84.8% * |
| 1999 | Criminal justice reform | CIR | 84.8% * |

*held concurrently with a general election

*Table 3.2* Referendums held between 2000–2020

| Year | Subject | Type | Turnout |
|---|---|---|---|
| 2009 | Child discipline law | CIR | 56.09% |
| 2011 | Retention of MMP | Government | 73.11%* |
| 2013 | Asset sales | CIR | 45.07% |
| 2015 | Flag change I | Government | 48.2% |
| 2016 | Flag change II | Government | 67.8% |
| 2020 | End of life choices | Government | 82.24%* |
| 2020 | Cannabis reform | Government | 82.24%* |

*held concurrently with a general election

The 2009 child discipline CIR Act referendum was the first to be held since the double CIR referendums in 1999. The impact of those referendums was to have caused (in New Zealand terms) significant delay to the return of the general election results and triggered a government review into the conduct of the count. It was perhaps this experience that led the Chief Electoral Officer to advise the Prime Minister that the child discipline vote should not be held in conjunction with the 2008 general election as it would "inevitably lead to voter confusion, congestion in polling places and put at risk the timing of the parliamentary count" (Trevett, 2008).

New Zealanders were initially very enthusiastic about the potential for increased direct democracy as enabled by the CIR Act. As I have written elsewhere (Morris, 2004, p.117),

in 1994, eighteen questions were submitted by seven different organisations and individuals. However, within one decade of the Act's coming into force, enthusiasm for citizen-initiated referendums seems to have waned considerably. In 2000, only three petition questions were submitted; two lapsed, and the other was withdrawn. In 2001 two questions were submitted; both have lapsed. In 2002, not one question was submitted.

This pattern has continued, with three petitions in 2003 and 2007, none in 2008, two in 2009, none in 2010, one each in 2011 and 2012, and then a long gap to 2018 when two petitions were submitted. One petition proposal each was submitted in 2020 and 2022, and two in 2023. Of this latter period, only two petitions of 12 have resulted in a referendum, with only one proposal open as of January 2024. This decline is probably not unrelated to the lack of meaningful or direct government action in relation to the results of the CIR referendums.

## When and how are referendums won or lost?

It is axiomatic that the success or failure of a referendum question is primarily determined by the level of popular support for the proposition. That is of course what a referendum primarily is designed to test. However, ancillary matters may also have some influence over the outcome. Voters may use the referendum as a way of expressing their support (or otherwise) for the ruling party or the state of politics in general; referendums may also be manipulated to some extent by those who set the rules of how and when they are conducted.

### *Government manipulation of referendum design*

#### *Government referendums*

Qvortrup (2000) is among those who have noted that referendums are not always solely focused on the acceptability of the question posed to the people. They may have other purposes, such as facilitating the political legacy of a particular leader or displacing political contests from their usual forum to another while still retaining influence over the outcome (Mendelsohn and Parkin, 2001, pp.2–3). McKay's (2021) recent study analysing referendum rules in New Zealand concludes "governments change referendums in unique ways depending on the political circumstances, including precedents set by earlier referendums." In particular, he notes that the serial alcohol polls and the multi-stage referendums were sites where this phenomenon was most likely to occur. In addition, rules such as turnout thresholds, or requirements for a super-majority or double referendum (Constitution Unit, 2018, p.110) can also serve to protect minority groups, enhance the legitimacy of the vote or lessen the likelihood of a particular result.

The triennial liquor referendums were an early example of this phenomenon. Earlier local polls had been subject to a 50% turnout requirement. This was removed for the national poll, and substituted with a requirement that the liquor referendum take place at the same time as the general election. This, McKay (2021, p.8) considers, along with the requirement for the prohibition option to secure at least 60% of the votes rather than a simple majority, was to ensure that prohibitionists could not benefit from lower general voter engagement with the issue. Further amendments to the alcohol referendums under the Licensing Amendment Act 1918, including the addition of the "state control" option (Christoffel, 2008, p.167) and the reduction of the approval threshold to 50% under Prime Minister William Massey reflected the decreasing threat represented by prohibitionists (McKay, p.9)—while they could still be satiated by having the question put to the public, after the 1919 poll the result was never in doubt. As the prohibition movement diminished in significance from the 1930s, the triennial alcohol poll became less important as a forum for political contest and attention turned elsewhere.

The 1992 and 1993 referendums provided the next opportunity for the government to use direct democracy as a way of purportedly seeking the will of the people while at the same time attempting to set the rules of the game in their favour. Roper and Leitch (1995, p.124) were of the view that "the suspicion remains that the Government intended to make the electoral reform process as difficult as possible. Certainly, FPTP was strongly supported by many Members of Parliament prior to the election." As McKay observes (2021, p.10):

> This referendum was widely seen as an attempt by the National government to reduce the odds that MMP would win. The first question on the first ballot provided a possible advantage to the government since a vote for FPTP would lead the government to abandon plans for the second, binding referendum, while a vote for change would give FPTP a second chance to prevail. The provision of four alternative systems allowed National to include options that they perceived as less harmful to their electoral prospects while potentially splitting the pro-reform vote.

This strategy did not work in the face of New Zealanders' disaffection with the current political system. It did, however, create a precedent for two further referendums: the second referendum in 2011 on the retention of MMP, and the vote on changing the national flag in 2015–2016. Both of these were designed as two-stage referendums. The MMP referendum proceeded according to the same pattern as the electoral reform referendums of the 1990s. However, the flag referendum reversed this pattern. Here, the Prime Minister did not wish to protect the status quo, but to change it. New Zealanders were asked first not whether they wanted a change in the flag, but what would they want to change to. It was only in the second referendum that New Zealanders voted on whether they wished to change the existing flag itself.

It could also be said that the precedential weight of a referendum also occurs in substantive areas (see Mendelsohn and Parkin, 2001, p.11). Having held one referendum on pub closing hours in 1949, it would have been difficult for the government to have changed the law without a reversal of the public view that liberalisation was not preferred. Accordingly, it was not until this was signalled in the referendum in 1967 that the government was able to introduce legislation to effect this change. Similarly, given that the public declined to agree to a longer parliamentary term in 1967, this could not be changed without their consent via referendum. A second attempt at the question in 1990 again resulted in a "no" vote, and the question has not featured again.

*Citizen Initiated Referenda Act referendums*

Referendums under the CIR Act are also subject to limitations on their effectiveness as a device for conveying the popular vote to elected representatives. The Act itself places a number of restrictions on the questions that may be the subject of a CIR referendum. Firstly, there can only be one question, and that it must be such that only one of two answers can be given (i.e., it must be capable of being answered with either "yes" or "no"). A question may not be asked where a referendum of "like effect" (left undefined by the CIR Act) has been held in the previous five years, nor may it concern an inquiry into the way a previous CIR Act referendum was conducted or an electoral petition under the Electoral Act 1993.

Assistance with the wording of the petition question is limited to the Clerk of the House of Representatives' role in ensuring that the question clearly conveys the purpose and effect of the proposal put forward by the promoter. Alternative drafts or wording clarifications are not permitted. Even this limited role has been problematic. After the 1994 *Egg Producers* case where the Clerk's power was challenged (see below), the light touch approach to using this power has led to a range of at times confusing, opaque, and vague questions being put to the New Zealand public. Take, for example the 1999 criminal justice referendum question which asked "should there be a reform of our Justice system placing greater emphasis on the needs of victims, providing restitution and compensation for them and imposing minimum sentences and hard labour for all serious violent offences?" Gendall et al. (2002, p.306) note that this compound question not only could be separated into five distinct questions, key matters such as the meaning of "restitution," "hard labour," and "serious violent offences" were left undefined and so were left up to individual interpretation. Similar charges can be laid against the "smacking" referendum, which asked "should a smack as part of good parental correction be a criminal offence in New Zealand?" leaving the meaning of the terms "smack" and "good parental correction" up to the voter to determine. This lack of certainty and intelligibility in the question breaks the link between the purported will of the people and its determination, allowing politicians to respond equivocally to the result, dismiss it as meaningless, or take little direct action (Walker, 2003, p.18).

Research into the "readability" (Gilliland, 1972, pp.89–93)—the relationship between comprehension and the complexity of the text—of New Zealand's referendum questions has shown that the average question performs poorly on both the Flesch Reading Ease Scale and the Gunning Fog Index (Morris, 2004, pp.123–124). The average question scores 17.4 on the Fog Index, indicating that several years of university education are required to understand the question properly. On the Flesch scale, where 65 represents plain English, and 0 represents text that is "extremely difficult to read", the average CIR question scores 27.12 (Goschzik, 2003, pp.722–723). This demonstrably low readability of the questions confronting the New Zealand voter cannot help the majority of voters to make an informed and sensible decision about the issues before them, both when asked to sign a petition and when voting.

A further barrier to the intelligibility of the question is the low ceiling of NZ$50,000 (approximately US$30,000 or €28,380 at the time of writing) placed on expenditure of advertising the petition or the referendum. Although this has the laudable aim of addressing the problem of any one group or individual using its financial resources to secure a disproportionate influence over the petition's success, such a small sum is quickly exhausted and relies on petition promoters and opponents who are in turn reliant on the media for publicity about the proposal, its meaning, and effects.

At an institutional level, assistance in understanding the question is also not forthcoming from the government. The New Zealand *Cabinet Manual* (2017, pp.120–121) states that Ministers should not become involved in CIR petitions or referendums without Cabinet approval and that "departments should avoid commenting publicly on the merits of referendum proposals unless they have the permission of the Minister to do so." Furthermore, government institutions have limited powers to assist with public understanding. Even when they do, their contribution cannot be guaranteed. The Electoral Commission was unable to provide an explanatory leaflet outlining both sides of the debate on the 1995 firefighters' referendum when the two sides were unable to come to an agreement on the wording (Boston, 2000, p.193). It did provide a pamphlet for the 1999 referendum on the number of MPs, although Boston (2000, p.193) points to the fact that it had a statutory duty to do so under the Electoral Act because it was categorised as an electoral matter. The Ministry of Justice, under no similar duty, contributed nothing in respect of the criminal justice referendum, also held in 1999.

### Elite interventions: Personal and institutional

New Zealand government institutions and officials tend to keep their distance from the referendum process. At times, this is rooted in the view that the processes of direct democracy should not be manipulated by representative politicians. New Zealanders tend to respond poorly to being told how to think by their elected representatives, displaying a degree of bloody-mindedness in response to statements issuing from political quarters.

For example, prior to the cannabis reform referendum, Prime Minister Jacinda Ardern refused to say how she would vote, citing the disproportionate influence her views might have on the outcome (Robinson, 2020). Analysis after the referendum was held suggested that this self-imposed silence may in fact, have influenced New Zealanders to vote against reform (Rychert and Wilkins, 2021, p.878). Arden later revealed that she had voted "yes" (Manch, 2020). Similarly, Prime Minister John Key did not comment on the 2011 electoral system referendum held during his previous term of government, perhaps mindful of the backlash against politicians that underpinned the vote for MMP in 1992 and 1993. Key and his opposite number, Phil Goff MP, also declined to say whether they would vote in the 2009 CIR Act child discipline vote (Young, 2009). This is not a uniform phenomenon however, as Key made no secret of his views that the flag should be changed as well as his preferred replacement (Robinson, 2020).

On other occasions, the reluctance to engage with referendum processes is more prosaic. The wording of the very first CIR petition ended up as the subject of litigation. The Act provides for the Clerk of the House of Representatives (a very senior public official). The original question formulated by the Society for the Prevention of Cruelty to Animals asked: "should the inhumane practice of battery hen production be phased out within five years from this referendum?" This was refined by the Clerk to read "should the production of eggs from battery hens be prohibited within five years of the referendum?'" The Egg Producers Federation took issue with the term "battery hens," claiming that it was not neutral and would influence the electorate to vote for abolition. A judicial review of the decision was brought (*Egg Producers Federation of NZ* v *Clerk of the House of Representatives*, 1994). Although the High Court upheld the Clerk's reformulation of the question, it is notable that subsequent petition questions have generally passed from the petitioner to the Clerk and back with no or little amendment. Parkinson (2001, p.420) also notes that in the case of the criminal justice referendum, "reading between the lines of the correspondence between the Clerk and Mr Withers … given the non-binding nature of the vote, the Clerk simply gave up fighting with a distrustful proponent."

By contrast, government-led referendums are subject to no official external scrutiny or input. This is unlike the situation in other similar jurisdictions such as the United Kingdom, where the Political Parties, Elections and Referendums Act 2000 assigns responsibility for the final determination of a referendum question to the UK's Electoral Commission (Constitution Unit, 2018, pp.101–102). Instead, New Zealand has experimented with a variety of ad hoc methods of disseminating knowledge and informing debate for government referendums. The two most-utilised methods are the independent panel and the public information programme.

The first instance of the public information programme occurred with the 1967 referendums on the term of parliament and the change to licensing hours with the delivery of a factual pamphlet on the options delivered to every New Zealand household. This was repeated in 1990 when the term of parliament was again the subject of a referendum (Cleveland and Robinson, 1972, pp.134–135).

The two MMP referendums in 1992 and 1993 were preceded by an extensive information campaign. The government-funded Electoral Referendum Panel (ERP) was set up to explain the electoral systems to be put to the public vote in "an objective, impartial and informative manner" (Levine and Roberts, 1994, p.243). Headed by the Chief Ombudsman, Sir John Robertson, the panel sought to contact every eligible voter in the country. For the 1992 two-stage election, the ERP created a brochure (in English, Māori, and Samoan) outlining the five different systems under consideration (FPTP, MMP, STV, SM, and PV) which was delivered to every household in New Zealand. A videotape was made to accompany the brochure. The ERP also made three television programmes about the referendum. There were also longer guides to the referendum and a series of seminars run throughout the country (Levine and Roberts, 1993, p.161). A similar approach was taken for the 1993 referendum between MMP and FPTP (Levine and Roberts, 1994, p.243). The ERP sent out a brochure for each household, a personalised letter and brochure to every registered elector, and an official 16-page guide to the referendum. Television advertisements supplemented the printed information drive.

Nearly 20 later, the 2011 referendum on MMP saw the Electoral Commission undertake a multi-media information campaign (Constitution Unit, 2018, p.166). The six-month long campaign included leaflets to every New Zealand household, television advertisements, online information, and DVDs about the upcoming referendum and the options that would be presented to voters. The Commission also devised a "referendum toolkit" which was an interactive web programme allowing voters to rank their preferred criteria to reveal which referendum option best aligned with those preferences (Arseneau and Roberts, 2012, p.331).

The public information campaign was again reverted to for New Zealand's most recent referendums, those on cannabis reform and assisted dying. Given the nature of the topics, responsibility for informing voters was given to the Ministry of Justice. The Ministry created a website (www.referendums.govt.nz) providing factual and impartial information on the two topics. In addition, the Ministry ran a multi-channel signposting campaign which included advertising online, on the radio, and outdoors (such as bus advertisements) directing people to the referendum website.

The other, less common approach, is the expert panel. This was first seen in relation to the 1999 referendum on a compulsory retirement saving scheme. The government appointed Sir John Robertson to reprise his role as the public face of referendum information, creating a perception of continued impartiality in the government. As with the ERP, the expert panel was to provide factual and objective information only to voters. The panel adopted a multi-media approach using television, brochures, radio, and the internet to communicate the issues around the referendum. Voters were also invited to write to or telephone specially set up information centres with technical questions. Finally, the panel gave a number of national and regional talks and presentations to specific interest groups such as the New Zealand Māori Council, the National Council of Women, and employer representatives (Preston, 1997, p.146).

The Flag Consideration Panel was set up to lead the public engagement process with the two-stage flag referendum. It had 12 members, drawn from a wide range of New Zealand society who were selected by a cross-party parliamentary group (the NZ First party declined to participate). In addition to the now-familiar requirements of objectivity and impartiality, the Flag Consideration Panel was also expected to ensure that the process was dignified, inclusive, and mindful of the position of the indigenous Māori people. A multi-media approach was again employed. In-person events were not well-attended but online engagement was significant. New Zealanders were invited to submit their own designs for a new flag—some of which were quite quirky and attracted international attention. The Panel eventually chose four designs to be voted on in the 2015 referendum. The official process was somewhat derailed when a public protest at the very similar nature of the four designs led to a successful parliamentary petition to include a fifth design with resultant last-minute legislation to allow that to happen (Jones, 2016).

### Other considerations

In other cases, referendums appear to have been the victim of low public interest in the subject matter. The November 2011 referendum on the electoral system had been on the public agenda for some time, but by the time it was held, the devastating Christchurch earthquake of February 2011 and the Rugby World Cup in October 2011 (hosted and won by New Zealand) had put political questions firmly into second or even third place as national priorities (Arseneau and Roberts, 2012, p.331). As Johansson and Levine (2012, p.15) comment, the impact of the latter was "probably difficult to comprehend to anyone not a New Zealander" rendering the referendum "if not an afterthought, at best something of a footnote" (Johansson and Levine, 2012, p.16).

There was a similar lack of interest in the referendums to change the flag. Trevett (2015) notes that the Flag Consideration Panel, appointed by the government at a cost of NZ$6.7 million to "design and lead the public engagement process" on the proposed change, spoke to an average audience of 29 people at its travelling roadshow around New Zealand. While turnout in both referendums was respectable, in each case, New Zealanders opted for the status quo rather than for change. It is worth noting, however, that support for referendums per se in New Zealand has not declined but has actually increased since the flag referendums (Greaves et al., 2021, p.140).

## The political and legal consequences of referendums

Referendums serve two distinct but overlapping purposes in New Zealand politics. The first reflects the traditional view, that referendums are a way of ascertaining the public will on issues that are too contentious or inappropriate for elected representatives to decide (Walker, 2008, p.11). The outcomes of these referendums are respected, and where appropriate, implemented, even when the referendum itself was not deemed to be binding. In this category, we can place the triennial liquor poll, the referendums on gambling, pub opening times, compulsory military training, the term of Parliament, changes to the electoral system, compulsory retirement savings, changing the national flag, cannabis reform, and assisted dying. All of these referendums were government-initiated.

We can also observe that the use of referendums created an expectation that certain types of questions requiring legislative change could only be revisited in the same way—and often for long periods. One such example is the national alcohol licencing referendums which ran from 1911 to 1987. Once the government had established the referendum as the device through which New Zealanders would decide, it became "cemented into New Zealand's political consciousness the notion that alcohol was so sensitive a subject that issues concerning it ought to be regularly put to the people in referendums" (Prince, 1996, p.56). Other changes to alcohol policy were also put to a referendum. This practice only came to a halt when the triennial licensing referendum was abandoned. A similar pattern can be observed with electoral reform. Despite the existence of statutory provisions allowing for changes to fundamental aspects of the electoral system to be made in the legislature via the super-majority process (see s 268 Electoral Act 1993), the questions of electoral reform and the term of parliament were put instead to the public vote. Thus referendums beget more referendums.

Perhaps not surprising, given New Zealand's uncodified and pragmatically-orientated constitutional arrangements, was the degree to which referendums were the result of ad hoc political decisions or the outcome of inter-party political bargains. This can be seen from the early days of the New Zealand experience. Outside of the triennial alcohol polls, the first referendums held in New Zealand came about due to divisions within the governing party which underpinned the first two referendums in 1949, and the third was made possible by a bargain struck between the two political parties in the legislature, where the opposition would support the government's two referendums in return for a promise to hold the third. After the adoption of MMP (itself by referendum), three coalition agreements have provided for the holding of a referendum: on a national retirement scheme in 1997, cannabis law reform in

2020, and the proposed referendum on the Treaty of Waitangi following the 2023 election.

The second is a more fluid understanding of the way in which politics is conducted. In this view, referendums are not simply an alternative means of deciding difficult questions. In New Zealand, referendums can also be seen as a way in which to (re)launch an item onto the policy agenda and as part of wider political debate and development. On this point, Catt (2001, p.390) argues that CIR petitions generally deal with matters of on-going public concern.

A referendum can sometimes respond to elite political action, especially legislation. Most of the CIR Act referendums fall into this category: the referendum on reducing the number of firefighters, the one on reducing the number of MPs, the vote on the removal of "reasonable chastisement of a child" as a defence to assault, and the referendum on the sale of national assets. In this scenario, the public (sometimes assisted or co-opted by political actors) begins a dialogue with the government, voicing their disapproval of political decisions, and seeking to open up the debate more widely to the general public for their input.

Although the propositions of the CIR Act referendums were strongly endorsed in four of the five votes, none has been implemented. However, that is not to say that no action resulted.

In the case of the two 1999 CIR Act referendums, the government took notice of the public voice and referred both issues for review. The question on the reduction of MPs to 99 was included in the terms of reference of a parliamentary selected committee reviewing the experience of MMP, and the criminal justice matters were also the subject of a government-led review (Parkinson, 2001, pp.418–419). In the latter case, some minor amendments were made to sentencing laws. In the former, recommendations were rendered virtually impossible to achieve by the requirement in the terms of reference for the MMP Review Committee that the committee make its recommendations by consensus. The child discipline referendum also resulted in a government review led by the Police and the Department of Child, Youth and Family of the change to the law to assess how it was working in practice.

An interesting outlier to this pattern is the 2011 government-initiated vote on the retention of MMP. Despite the public voting to retain MMP, the enabling legislation for the referendum provided that should MMP win, a review would be conducted by the Electoral Commission. This took place in 2012. Some minor amendments were proposed. However, nothing was implemented, since, in a repeat of the lack of consensus on MMP seen in the 2001 parliamentary committee review, agreement between parliamentary parties could not be achieved (Chapman, 2013).

Political responses to citizen-initiated referendums can also occur prospectively (Gerber and Hug in Mendelsohn and Parkin, 2001, p.90). Prior to the 1999 criminal justice referendum, the National government attempted some reform in an attempt to stave off the venting of public disquiet via the vote. Fast-tracked legislation provided for longer sentences for aggravated robberies and longer non-parole periods of serious offenders (Church, 2000, p.193). Later that year, the government also introduced the Victims' Rights Bill (enacted in 2002) which included guidance on the treatment of victims and requiring victim impact statements to be given more weight. Other parties made law and order issues a feature of their campaign in various ways, from endorsing restorative justice measures (Labour) to calling for sentences of "hard labour" to be imposed (NZ First) to requiring offenders to serve at least 80% of their sentence (ACT) (Church, 2000, p.193). Unsurprisingly, politicians were mute on the question of whether there should be fewer MPs.

In addition to becoming a feature of post-election party bargaining, referendums themselves can also stimulate more political activity and development. At least two political parties can link their beginnings in direct democracy, one post-referendum and one pre-referendum.

Following the failure of the government to implement the result of the reduction of MP numbers, and the subsequent refusal of the MMP Review Committee to agree that MP numbers should be reduced, the 99 MP Party was created in 2001. The idea for the party came from a local Wellington businessman who then became party leader for a short time before being replaced by Margaret Robertson. Party policies put forward including parliamentary reform and a strengthening of the criminal law, reflecting the public support for both CIR Act referendums in 1999. The party did not contest the 2002 election, but was officially registered for the 2005 election where it obtained 0.03% of the vote. It was deregistered in 2006. The brief existence of the 99 MP Party may have stimulated the introduction of a private member's (i.e., non-government sponsored) bill in March 2006 to reduce the number of MPs to 100.

Similarly short-lived was the Kiwi Party, set up in 2007 by two members of Parliament dissatisfied by their party's support for the changes to the Crimes Act on disciplining children. One of the founder MPs was then a co-sponsor of the 2009 CIR Act referendum challenging the amendment. The Kiwi Party contested the 2008 election on a platform of fiscal reform and the holding of an inquiry into domestic violence and child abuse, winning 0.54% of the popular vote. It contested a by-election in 2009 and announced plans to contest the 2011 general election but this did not happen. Instead, its members, including the co-founders, formed an alliance with the Conservative Party and stood under their label. The Conservative Party (rebranded as the New Conservatives from 2017) also advocated a socially conservative platform, including repeal of the 2007 change to the Crimes Act on the physical chastisement of children. The Kiwi Party was deregistered in 2012. The Conservative Party continues to exist. It has put forward candidates at all general elections between 2014 and 2023 . Literature on the party website still refers to the amendment to the Crimes Act as evidence of the lack of government integrity.

## Conclusion

The frequency of referendums in New Zealand can in part be explained by its practice of holding (most of its) referendums to coincide with its triennial general elections. By using the electoral infrastructure and staffing already in place, advantage can be taken of the fact that filling out a second ballot paper requires little effort. Both participation and legitimacy of the result are enhanced this way. New Zealand has also been a frequent practitioner of the multi-stage/multi-option referendum which challenges the usual objections to referendums as "blunt and crude devices" (RCES, 1986, p.175). New Zealand also has the advantage of being a small country where the populace is easy to reach and inform of the issues at stake both through public information campaigns and travelling expert panels.

As Butler and Ranney (1994, p.258) observed in their global survey of referendums nearly two decades ago, "[all] referendums are unique, both in origins and in consequences" and the same can be said of the response, which this study shows is typically closely tied to the circumstances and history of the nation. The vote to change the electoral system in 1992 and 1993 reflected a very difficult, and for some, painful, political era in New Zealand's political history where politicians governed autocratically, even illegally,[1] and political alienation increased significantly. The lukewarm response to the 2011 referendum asking whether the new electoral system should be retained can be directly attributed to the national experience of 2011, a year that began with a devastating earthquake and ended with a nation-affirming sporting victory.

Lastly, the role of referendums in New Zealand society has evolved some way from the traditional understanding of direct democracy as a supplement or replacement for representative democracy. Referendums have been used to assert a dissatisfied citizen voice with existing or forthcoming legislative changes as well as becoming part of the armoury of inter-party coalition negotiations.

## References

Arseneau, T. and Roberts, N. (2012). '"Kicking the Tyres on MMP": The Results of the Referendum Reviewed', In Johansson, J. and Levine, S. (eds). *Kicking the Tyres – The New Zealand General Election and Electoral Referendum of 2011*. Wellington: Victoria University Press. pp.325–346.

Boston, J., Church, S., Levine, S. and McLeay, E. (eds) (2000). *Left Turn: The New Zealand General Election of 1999*. Wellington: Victoria University Press.

1 See *Fitzgerald* v *Muldoon* [1976] 2 NZLR 615 where the Prime Minister Robert Muldoon attempted to make changes to a superannuation (pension) scheme via executive fiat in the form of a press release when legislative action was required to do so. The court declared his actions to have no legal effect.

Butler, D. and Ranney, A. (eds) (1994). *Referendums Around the World*. Basingstoke: Palgrave Macmillan.

Catt, H. (2001). 'Citizens Initiated Referenda', In Miller, R. (ed). *New Zealand Government and Politics*. Auckland: Oxford University Press. pp.386–395.

Chapman, K. (2013). *Government's MMP Review Response Slammed*. Available at: https://www.stuff.co.nz/national/8674192/Governments-MMP-review-response -slammed (Accessed: 22 January 2024).

Christoffel, P. (2008). 'Prohibition and the Myth of 1919', *New Zealand Journal of History*, 42(2), pp.154–175.

Church, S. (2000). 'Crime and Punishment: The Referenda to Reform the Criminal Justice System and Reduce the Size of Parliament', in Boston, J., Church, S., Levine, S. and McLeay, E. (eds). *Left Turn: The New Zealand General Election of 1999*. Wellington: Victoria University Press. pp.184–199.

Cleveland, L. and Robinson, A.D. (eds) (1972). *Readings in New Zealand Government*. Wellington: Reed Publishing.

Constitution Unit. (2018). *Report of the Independent Commission on Referendums*. London: UCL.

*Egg Producers Federation of NZ v Clerk of the House of Representatives*, HC Wellington CP128/94, 20 June 1994.

Gendall, P., Hoek, J. and Willis, A. (2002). 'Respondent Understanding of the 1999 Referendum Question on a Reform of the New Zealand Justice System', *Australian Journal of Political Science*, 37(2), pp.303–315.

Gerber, E.R. and Hug, S. (2001). 'Legislative Responses to Direct Legislation', In Mendelsohn, M. and Parkin, A. (eds). *Referendum Democracy*. Basingstoke: Palgrave Macmillan, 88–108.

Gilliland, J. (1972). *Readability*. London: University of London Press.

Goschik, B. (2003). 'You're The Voice – Try and Understand it: Some Practical Problems of the Citizens Initiated Referenda Act', *Victoria University of Wellington Law Review*, 34(4), p.695–727.

Greaves, L.M., Oldfield, L.D. and Milne, B.J. (2021). 'Let the People Decide? Support for Referenda since the New Zealand Flag Change Referendums', *Kōtuitui: New Zealand Journal of Social Sciences Online*, 16(1), pp.1–15.

Johansson, J. and Levine, S. (eds) (2012). *Kicking the Tyres – The New Zealand General Election and Electoral Referendum of 2011*. Wellington: Victoria University Press.

Jones, A. (2016). 'The Tangled Tale of New Zealand's Flag Debate', *BBC News,* 24 March. Available at: https://www.bbc.co.uk/news/world-asia-35878485 (Accessed: 22 January 2024).

Levine, S. and Roberts, N.S. (1993). 'The New Zealand Electoral Referendum of 1992', *Electoral Studies*, 12(2), pp.158–167.

Levine, S. and Roberts, N.S. (1994). 'The New Zealand Electoral Referendum and General Election of 1993', *Electoral Studies*, 13(3), pp.240–253.

Manch, T. (2020). 'Referendum Results: Prime Minister Jacinda Ardern Voted 'Yes' for Both Cannabis and Euthanasia', *Stuff,* 30 October. Available at: https://www.stuff .co.nz/national/politics/123252994/referendum-results-prime-minister-jacinda -ardern-voted-yes-for-both-cannabis-and-euthanasia?fbclid=IwAR0hA_fwd1VSN kN9Uqn8YbYk5TlcKmJoBklt_jVHynH9gy4YpIeU7uqMCqk (Accessed: 22 January 2024).

McKay, S. (2021). 'The Politics of Referendum Rules: Evidence from New Zealand (1893 – 2016)', *Politics & Policy*, pp.1–17.

Mendelsohn, M. and Parkin, A. (eds) (2001). *Referendum Democracy*. Basingstoke: Palgrave Macmillan.

Morris, C. (2004). 'Improving Our Democracy or a Fraud on the Community? A Closer Look at New Zealand's Citizens Initiated Referenda Act 1993', *Statute Law Review*, 25(2), pp.116–135.

New Zealand Government. (2017). *Cabinet Manual*. Wellington: Department of the Prime Minister and Cabinet.

Parkinson, J. (2001). 'Who Knows Best? The Creation of the Citizen-initiated Referendum in New Zealand', *Government and Opposition*, 36(3), pp.403–422.

Preston, D.A. (1997). 'The Compulsory Retirement Savings Scheme Referendum of 1997', *Social Policy Journal of NZ*, 9, pp.138–150.

Prince, J.L. (1996). 'Look Back in Amber: The General Licensing Poll in New Zealand, 1919-87', *Political Science*, 48(1), pp.48–72.

Qvortrup, M. (2000). 'Are Referendums Controlled and Pro-Hegemonic?', *Political Studies*, 48(4), pp.821–826.

Robinson, C. (2020). 'How the Wider Political Agenda Risks Skewing New Zealand's Cannabis Referendum', *The Guardian*, 12 October. Available at: https://www.theguardian.com/commentisfree/2020/oct/12/how-the-wider-political-agenda-risks-skewing-new-zealands-cannabis-referendum (Accessed: 22 January 2024).

Roper, J. and Leitch, S. (1995). 'The Electoral Reform Campaigns in New Zealand: A Political Communication Case Study', *The Australian Journal of Communication*, 22(1), pp.123–135.

Royal Commission on the Electoral System. (1986). *Report of the Royal Commission on the Electoral System: Towards a Better Democracy*. Available at: https://web.archive.org/web/20170524153410/http://www.elections.org.nz/voting-system/mmp-voting-system/report-royal-commission-electoral-system-1986 (Accessed: 22 January 2024).

Rychert, M. and Wilkins, C. (2021). 'Why did New Zealand's Referendum to Legalise Recreational Cannabis Fail?', *Drug and Alcohol Review*, 40, pp.877–881.

Trevett, C. (2008). 'Smack Referendum Next Year, Says Clark', *NZ Herald*, 25 June. Available at: https://www.nzherald.co.nz/nz/smack-referendum-next-year-says-clark-video/YUUPECHDZ2BRUUFGDAGLIJFHOA/?c_id=1501165&objectid=10518391 (Accessed: 22 January 2024).

Trevett, C. (2015). 'Flag Show at Half Mast', *NZ Herald*, 17 July. Available at: https://www.nzherald.co.nz/nz/flag-show-at-half-mast/2WZJ3TYQAILVKQPTK27DJHCMC4/?c_id=1500876&objectid=11482801 (Accessed: 22 January 2024).

Walker, M. (2003). *The Strategic Use of Referendums: Power, Legitimacy, and Democracy*. New York: Palgrave Macmillan.

Young, A. (2009). 'Big Two Coy on Smacking Vote', *NZ Herald*, 16 June. Available at: https://www.nzherald.co.nz/nz/politics/big-two-coy-on-smacking-vote/IVL7WGDRB56ARG3RB4FFSET3DU/?c_id=144&objectid=10578914 (Accessed: 22 January 2024).

# 4 Conclusion

## Introduction

It has been said (Gordon, 2020: p.216) that direct democracy "is arguably always idiosyncratic" and it would be remiss not to acknowledge this point here. And of course, the New Zealand political experience cannot be exactly replicated elsewhere. Nonetheless, there are useful observations to be made as a result of this study. What can New Zealand teach us about referendums and small state democracy?

## A different understanding of the referendum

Firstly, Linder and Mueller (2021, p.131) claim that different types of direct democracy measures have different effects, stating that "the referendum has a 'braking' effect and the [citizens'] initiative an innovative one." This study of New Zealand disturbs this distinction by reversing it. In New Zealand we see the government referendum being used to promote change in the form of bringing in legal reforms, such as new alcohol licencing regimes, changing the electoral system, drug decriminalisation or introducing assisted dying. We also see citizen-initiated referendums being employed to challenge reforms, such as laws outlawing the smacking of children or the sales of national assets or to seek a return to the status quo as with the referendum on reducing the number of MPs, or returning the fire service to particular staffing levels. This distinction reflects the traditional history of the New Zealand government as a reformist and innovative one—one perhaps sometimes too radical and fast-moving for its people.

We also see in New Zealand a willingness to innovate and experiment with the referendum. This flexibility is in part allowed by New Zealand's uncodified constitution. But it also comes from its longstanding use of the referendum as New Zealand has had the luxury both of time and repeated use of the referendum in which to make it fit for purpose. This agility and flexibility in public policy choices and law is also an often-noted characteristic of the small state (Baldacchino, 2018, p.4), one which is not hindered by multiple levels

DOI: 10.4324/9781003472452-4

of government and bi-cameral legislatures, or held back by large bureaucracies. We see this dynamism in practice in New Zealand where referendums have been held in person and by post. They have asked one question or several. Some are one-off events, others are staggered, with a second referendum depending on the result of the first. Some were held alongside general elections, others were standalone events. The introduction of the Citizens Initiated Referenda Act (CIR Act) allowing members of the public to propose the holding of a referendum on virtually any topic was an innovation not seen in the Commonwealth until its appearance in New Zealand.

In recent years, the trend in referendum design has been towards facilitating citizen understanding and participation, accompanied by extensive public information and engagement campaigns. Tierney (2013, pp.13–14) comments favourably on New Zealand's use of the multi-stage/multi-option referendum:

> [it] enhances participation by allowing citizens to take part in two separate constitutional events. It can also facilitate a longer period of public reasoning by extending the time available for reflection and discussion, as voters have a second referendum to address the issue anew with a narrower range of options.

The two most recent referendums held in 2020 asked simple questions on complex topics: assisted dying and cannabis decriminalisation. Both referendums adopted the practice of the earlier 1993 referendum on electoral reform by asking voters to endorse or reject a particular piece of legislation, eliminating uncertainty and thereby making it very clear exactly what voters were deciding on. While this latter has been a long-established referendum practice, as seen in Switzerland and as advocated by Dicey, it is the combining of this with the multi-stage referendum as seen in the electoral reform referendums which is unusual and worthy of greater consideration by other practitioners of the referendum.

### A new type of (referendum) democracy?

Linder and Mueller (2021, p.137) state that "direct success in a popular vote is rare," although they go on to note that a "failed" referendum vote may nonetheless push the government to give the idea more serious consideration, or to take it into account in already-existing legislative projects. The government response to referendums in New Zealand has exhibited a pendulum effect: when a proposition in a government-initiated referendum is endorsed, the vote is implemented forthwith (as with the votes on assisted dying, electoral reform, pub opening hours, and compulsory military training); when it is an advisory CIR Act referendum question that is endorsed, the response, if any, is minimal such as in the form of a review (as with the CIR results on the number of MPs) or minor legislative change (the CIR criminal justice referendum) or there is no response at all (the CIR Act referendums on firefighter numbers, child discipline, and asset sales all falling into this category).

Linder and Mueller also note (p.137–138) that "political parties and social movements can use the popular initiative as a platform for electoral success." Attempts to do this in New Zealand have failed, with no new political party promoting increased use of referendums or having its origins in referendum episode having any sort of electoral success. What we have seen is the reverse of this phenomenon. Established parties have been behind at least two, and possibly three, government referendums as well as at least three CIR Act referendums. Previously confined to central government, this use of the referendum has also recently emerged within local government as well and as we have seen, the decision to enact a law allowing for citizen-initiated referendums can be traced back to the pro-direct democracy individuals in the ruling National Party (themselves influenced by pressure groups, who in a small jurisdiction have more immediate and closer access to politicians).

Outside the frame of organised party politics, New Zealand's small, strongly personalised polity and population also influenced the holding of a number of referendums. Alcohol licencing referendums came into being due to the personal views (both on democracy and alcohol consumption) of two Premiers in the 1890s, while over a hundred years later, three referendums— assisted dying in 2020, and the state of the criminal justice system, and the number of MPs in 1999—resulted from the personal experiences of three ordinary individual New Zealanders. In the same timeframe, two government referendums, one on changing the flag and the other on compulsory retirement savings, came about because of the personal convictions of the Prime Minister and Deputy Prime Minister respectively.

## Conclusion

New Zealand initially adopted the referendum primarily as a means to determine difficult political questions. This is seen in the alcohol polls first held in the late 19th century which had their genesis in the desire of politicians to avoid offending both the prohibitionist movement and the growing liquor trade. Although there was no constitution providing for the holding of referendums and no history of direct democracy practices inherited from the colonial power, this was no barrier to their use (thus displacing Anckar's (2020) hypothesis that former British colonies did not adopt the referendum as part of their political practices). Also of note is the long-recurring nature, the first national referendum taking place in 1911 and the most recent in 2020. Referendums were thus bedded into the New Zealand constitutional culture and practice from the early days of nationhood. That said, referendums have not replaced representative democracy as the main form of New Zealand political decision-making. Referendums tend to come in clusters, several decades apart, and, in the case of government referendums put to the people high-level moral or constitutional questions, in keeping with their status as devices of "last-resort."

But, as this exploration of the New Zealand experience shows, the role of the referendum in New Zealand politics has varied considerably over the last century of use. This use appears closely tied to form. As noted, on the government side, direct democracy has typically been used to decide significant questions of public policy: whether alcohol sales should be prohibited, whether a new electoral system should be adopted, and whether the terminally ill should be allowed assistance to die. While referendum-promoting parties have not flourished in New Zealand, referendums themselves have become part of the political toolkit. When used by citizens (and sometimes, more or less overtly, opposition political parties) it has generally been used, sometimes successfully, as a form of protest against unpopular policies and laws: the sale of national assets, the increase in politicians required by MMP, the perceived deficiencies of the criminal justice system, and whether parents are able to discipline their children with "reasonable force."

As Corbett and Veenendaal (2018) claim, in a small state, politics takes on a hyper-personalised form, where individuals can have much greater sway over political events than in a larger state, the line between the private and public spheres is blurred, and the people have much closer and direct relationships with their representatives. While their research focused on representative democracy, through this study of a small state with an experience of referendums that exceeds most others globally, we can see that these claims apply no less to direct democracy too.

## References

Anckar, D. (2020). 'Small States: Politics and Policies', In Baldacchino, G. and Wivers, A. (eds). *Handbook on the Politics of Small States*. Cheltenham: Edward Elgar. pp.38–54.

Baldacchino, G. (2018). 'Mainstreaming Small States and Territories', *Small States and Territories,* 1(1), pp.3–16.

Corbett, J. and Veenendaal, W.P. (2018). *Democracy in Small States: Persisting Against All Odds*. Oxford: Oxford University Press.

Gordon, M. (2020). 'Referendums in the UK Constitution: Authority, Sovereignty and Democracy after Brexit', *European Constitutional Law Review*, 16, pp.213–243.

Linder, W. and Mueller, S. (2021). *Swiss Democracy*. Berlin: Springer.

Tierney, S. (2013). 'The Multi-option Referendum: International Guidelines, International Practice and Practical Issues'. University of Edinburgh Research Paper Series. 2013/33.

# Appendices

**Appendix I**

*Nationwide (non-licensing) referendums 1949–2023*

| Date | Form | Subject | Question | Votes in favour[a] | Turnout of Electorate | Mechanism |
|---|---|---|---|---|---|---|
| 9 March 1949 | Single question | Off-course betting | Proposal that provision be made for off-course betting on horse-races, through the totalizator, by means to be provided by the New Zealand Racing Conference and the New Zealand Trotting Conference | | 54.3% | Gaming Poll Act 1948 |
| | | | • I vote for the proposal | 68% | | |
| | | | • I vote against the proposal | 32% | | |
| 9 March 1949 | Single question | Extending hours for the sale of liquor | The proposed hours during which hotels shall be open for the sale of liquor are as follows: Hotels to be open, as at present, between 9 a.m. and 6 p.m. or for a total of nine hours, at times to be decided, between 10 a.m. and 10 p.m. | | 54.7% | Licensing Amendment Act 1948 |
| | | | • I vote for closing at 6 p.m. | 75.5% | | |
| | | | • I vote for closing at 10 p.m. | 24.5% | | |
| 3 August 1949 | Single question[b] | Compulsory military training | • I vote for compulsory military training | 77.9% | 63.5% | Military Training Poll Act 1949; Military Training Act 1949 |
| | | | • I vote against compulsory military training | 22.1% | | |
| 23 September 1967 | Single question | Three-year parliamentary term | Poll on Proposal to Change the Term of Parliament | | 69.7% | Electoral Poll Act 1967 |

| Date | Question type | Topic | Question / options | | Result | Relevant Act |
|---|---|---|---|---|---|---|
| | | | • I vote for a maximum of three years as at present | 68.1% | | |
| | | | • I vote for a maximum of four years | 31.9% | | |
| 23 September 1967 | Single question | Extending hours for the sale of liquor | Poll on Closing Hours for Sale of Liquor in Hotels, Taverns and Chartered Clubs | | 69.6% | Sale of Liquor Poll Act 1967; Sale of Liquor Amendment Act (No 2) 1967 |
| | | | • I favour 6 p.m. closing as at present | 35.6% | | |
| | | | • I favour later closing, the actual hours of sale to be decided according to local conditions | 64.5% | | |
| 27 October 1990 | Single question | Three-year parliamentary term^c | Poll on Proposal to Change the Term of Parliament | | 82.4% | Term Poll Act 1990 |
| | | | • I vote for 3 years as the term of Parliament as at present | 69.3% | | |
| | | | • I vote for 4 years as the term of Parliament | 30.7% | | |
| 19 September 1992 | Multi-stage and multi-option question(s) | 1. Voting system | Should New Zealand keep the First-Past-the-Post (FPTP) voting system? | | 55.2% | Electoral Referendum Act 1991 |
| | | | • I vote to retain the present First-Past-the-Post system | 15.3% | | |
| | | | • I vote for a change to the voting system | 84.7% | | |
| | | 2. Alternative voting system if system changed | If New Zealand were to change to another voting system, which voting system would you choose? | | | |
| | | | • Supplementary Member System | 5.6% | | |
| | | | • Single Transferable Vote | 17.4% | | |
| | | | • Mixed Member Proportional (MMP) | 70.5% | | |
| | | | • Preferential Voting | 6.6% | | |

*(Continued)*

*Appendix 1* (Continued)

| Date | Form | Subject | Question | Votes in favour[a] | Turnout of Electorate | Mechanism |
|---|---|---|---|---|---|---|
| 6 November 1993 | Multi-stage question | Change to MMP voting system[d] | • I vote for the present First-Past-The-Post System as provided in the Electoral Act 1956<br>• I vote for the proposed Mixed Member Proportional System as provided in the Electoral Act 1993 | 46.1%<br><br>53.9% | 82.6% | Electoral Referendum Act 1993; Electoral Act 1993 |
| 26 September 1997 | Single question | Proposed compulsory retirement savings scheme | Do you support the proposed compulsory retirement savings scheme? | 8.2% | 80.3% | Compulsory Retirement Savings Scheme Referendum Act 1997 |
| 26 November 2011 | Multi-stage and multi-option questions(s) | 1. Voting system<br>2. Alternative voting system if system changed | Should New Zealand keep the Mixed Member Proportional (MMP) voting system?<br>If New Zealand were to change to another voting system, which voting system would you choose?<br>• First-Past-the-Post<br>• Preferential Voting<br>• Single Transferable Vote<br>• Supplementary Member System | 56.2%<br><br><br>46.7%<br>12.5%<br>16.7%<br>24.1% | 73.5% | Electoral Referendum Act 2010 |
| 15 December 2015 | Multi-option question | First Referendum on the New Zealand Flag | If the New Zealand flag changes, which flag would you prefer?<br>• Silver Fern (Black, White and Blue)<br>• Red Peak<br>• Koru<br>• Silver Fern (Black and White)<br>• Silver Fern (Red, White and Blue) | 40.15%[c]<br>8.77%<br>3.78%<br>5.66%<br>41.64% | 48.8% | New Zealand Flag Referendums Act 2015 |

| Date | Type of question | Referendum | Question | Result | Turnout | Legislation |
|---|---|---|---|---|---|---|
| 30 March 2016 | Multi-option question | Second Referendum on the New Zealand Flag | What is your choice for the New Zealand flag?<br>• Silver Fern Flag<br>• Current New Zealand Flag | 43.2%<br>56.6% | 67.8% | New Zealand Flag Referendums Act 2015 |
| 17 October 2020 | Single question | End of Life Choice Referendum | Do you support the End of Life Choice Act 2019 coming into force? | 65.1%[f] | 81.9% | Referendums Framework Act 2019; End of Life Choice Act 2019 |
| 17 October 2020 | Single question | Cannabis Referendum | Do you support the proposed Cannabis Legalisation and Control Bill? | 48.4%[g] | 81.9% | Referendums Framework Act 2019 |

[a] As a percentage of valid votes cast.
[b] No specific question was asked. Voters were instructed to strike out one option, leaving untouched the option they wished to vote for.
[c] The alternative was a four-year term.
[d] No specific question was asked. Voters were instead given instructions on how to vote and provided with an explanation on the practical (including legislative) impact for either outcome.
[e] Voters were given a choice of five alternative flag options. The winner—Option A: Silver Fern (Black, White and Blue)—received 40.15% of the vote on the first count and 50.58% of the final vote following redistribution.
[f] https://electionresults.govt.nz/electionresults_2020/referendums-results.html
[g] https://electionresults.govt.nz/electionresults_2020/referendums-results.html

**Appendix II**

*Alcohol Licensing Referendums 1894–1987*

| Date | Form | Subject | Question | Votes in favour | Turnout of Electorate | Mechanism |
|---|---|---|---|---|---|---|
| 21 March 1894 | Multi-option poll[a] | Liquor licenses in local districts | Whether the present number of licenses is to continue ("continuance") | 39.5% | 47.1% | Alcohol Liquor Sale Control Act 1893 |
| | | | Whether the number is to be reduced ("reduction") | 15% | | |
| | | | Whether any licenses are to be granted ("no license") | 45.6% | | |
| 4 December 1896 | Multi-option poll[b] | Liquor licenses in local districts | Whether the present number of licenses is to continue ("continuance") | 53.7% | 76.6% | Alcohol Liquor Sale Control Act 1893 |
| | | | Whether the number is to be reduced ("reduction") | 36.4% | | |
| | | | Whether any licenses are to be granted ("no license") | 37.8% | | |
| 6 December 1899 | Multi-option poll[c] | Liquor licenses in local districts | Whether the number of licenses existing in the district shall continue? ("continuance") | 50.4% | 76.4% | Alcohol Liquor Sale Control Act 1893 |
| | | | Whether the number shall be reduced? ("reduction") | 38.4% | | |
| | | | Whether any licenses whateverr shall be granted? ("no license") | 42.2% | | |
| 25 November 1902 | Multi-option poll[d] | Liquor licenses in local districts | Whether the number of licenses existing in the district shall continue? ("continuance") | 46.6% | 76.7% | Alcohol Liquor Sale Control Act 1893 |

| Date | Poll type | Subject | Question | Result | Total | Legislation |
|---|---|---|---|---|---|---|
| | | | Whether the number shall be reduced? ("reduction") | 41.5% | | |
| | | | Whether any licenses whatsoever shall be granted? ("no license") | 47.5% | | |
| 6 December 1905 | Multi-option poll[e] | Liquor licenses in local districts | Whether the number of licenses existing in the district shall continue? ("continuance") | 46.1% | 83.2% | Alcohol Liquor Sale Control Act 1893 |
| | | | Whether the number shall be reduced? ("reduction") | 38.1% | | |
| | | | Whether any licenses whatever shall be granted? ("no license") | 50.1% | | |
| 17 November 1908 | Multi-option poll[f] | Liquor licenses in local districts | Whether the number of licenses existing in the district shall continue ("continuance") | 44.6% | 78.6% | Alcohol Liquor Sale Control Act 1893 |
| | | | Whether the number shall be reduced ("reduction") | 38.5% | | |
| | | | Whether any licenses whatever shall be granted? ("no license") | 52.5% | | |
| 7 and 14 December 1911 | Single question | Alcohol licensing | I vote against National Prohibition | 44.2% | 78.8% | Licensing Amendment Act 1910[g] |
| | | | I vote for National Prohibition | 55.8%[h] | | |
| | Single question | Liquor licenses in local districts | Whether the number of licenses existing in the district shall continue? ("continuance") | 50.3% | 83.5% | Licensing Amendment Act 1910 |
| | | | Whether any licenses whatever shall be granted? ("no license") | 49.7% | | |

*(Continued)*

*Appendix 11* (Continued)

| Date | Form | Subject | Question | Votes in favour | Turnout of Electorate | Mechanism |
|---|---|---|---|---|---|---|
| 10 December 1914 | Single question | Alcohol licensing | I vote against National Prohibition<br>I vote for National Prohibition | 51%<br>49% | 81.9% | Licensing Amendment Act 1910 |
| | Single question | Liquor licenses in local districts | Whether the number of licenses existing in the district shall continue? ("continuance")<br>Whether any licenses whatever shall be granted? ("no license") | 54.5%<br>45.6% | 81.8% | Licensing Amendment Act 1910 |
| 10 April 1919 | Single question | Alcohol licensing | For national continuance<br>For national prohibition with compensation | 51%<br>49% | 82.7% | Licensing Amendment Act 1918[i] |
| 17 December 1919 | Multi-option poll | Alcohol licensing | For national continuance<br>For state purchase and control<br>For national prohibition | 44.4%<br>5.9%<br>49.7% | 79.6% | Licensing Amendment Act 1918[i] |
| 7 December 1922 | Multi-option poll | Alcohol licensing | For national continuance<br>For state purchase and control<br>For national prohibition | 45.7%<br>5.8%<br>48.6% | 88.5% | Licensing Amendment Act 1910; Licensing Amendment Act 1918 |
| 4 November 1925 | Multi-option poll | Alcohol licensing | For national continuance<br>For state purchase and control<br>For national prohibition | 44.4%<br>8.3%<br>47.3% | 89.5% | Licensing Amendment Act 1910; Licensing Amendment Act 1918 |

| Date | Poll type | Topic | Options | % | Total % | Act |
|---|---|---|---|---|---|---|
| 14 November 1928 | Multi-option poll | Alcohol licensing | For national continuance<br>For state purchase and control<br>For national prohibition | 51%<br>8.8%<br>40.2% | 86.7% | Licensing Amendment Act 1910; Licensing Amendment Act 1918 |
| 27 November 1935 | Multi-option poll | Alcohol licensing | For national continuance<br>For state purchase and control<br>For national prohibition | 63.4%<br>7%<br>29.6% | 89.3% | Licensing Amendment Act 1910; Licensing Amendment Act 1918 |
| 15 October 1938 | Multi-option poll | Alcohol licensing | For national continuance<br>For state purchase and control<br>For national prohibition | 60.4%<br>10.6%<br>29% | 91.1% | Licensing Amendment Act 1910; Licensing Amendment Act 1918 |
| 25 September 1943 | Multi-option poll | Alcohol licensing | For national continuance<br>For state purchase and control<br>For national prohibition | 57.4%<br>13.4%<br>29.2% | 90.4% | Licensing Amendment Act 1910; Licensing Amendment Act 1918 |
| 27 November 1946 | Multi-option poll | Alcohol licensing | For national continuance<br>For state purchase and control<br>For national prohibition | 54%<br>20.2%<br>25.8% | 92.9% | Licensing Amendment Act 1910; Licensing Amendment Act 1918 |
| 30 November 1949 | Multi-option poll | Alcohol licensing | For national continuance<br>For state purchase and control<br>For national prohibition | 62%<br>12.8%<br>25.2% | 92.7% | Licensing Amendment Act 1910; Licensing Amendment Act 1918 |
| 13 November 1954 | Multi-option poll | Alcohol licensing | For national continuance<br>For state purchase and control<br>For national prohibition | 61.9%<br>15.1%<br>23% | 89.9% | Licensing Amendment Act 1910; Licensing Amendment Act 1918 |
| 30 November 1957 | Multi-option poll | Alcohol licensing | For national continuance<br>For state purchase and control<br>For national prohibition | 63.2%<br>14%<br>22.8% | 91.3% | Licensing Amendment Act 1910; Licensing Amendment Act 1918 |

(*Continued*)

*Appendix II* (Continued)

| Date | Form | Subject | Question | Votes in favour | Turnout of Electorate | Mechanism |
|---|---|---|---|---|---|---|
| 26 November 1960 | Multi-option poll | Alcohol licensing | For national continuance | 66% | 88.9% | Licensing Amendment Act 1910; Licensing Amendment Act 1918 |
| | | | For state purchase and control | 12% | | |
| | | | For national prohibition | 22% | | |
| 30 November 1963 | Multi-option poll | Alcohol licensing | For national continuance | 66.8% | 89% | Licensing Amendment Act 1910; Licensing Amendment Act 1918 |
| | | | For state purchase and control | 13.3% | | |
| | | | For national prohibition | 19.9% | | |
| 26 November 1966 | Multi-option poll | Alcohol licensing | For national continuance | 68.5% | 85.3% | Licensing Amendment Act 1910; Licensing Amendment Act 1918 |
| | | | For state purchase and control | 14.8% | | |
| | | | For national prohibition | 16.7% | | |
| 29 November 1969 | Multi-option poll | Alcohol licensing | For national continuance | 68.4% | 87.6% | Licensing Amendment Act 1910; Licensing Amendment Act 1918 |
| | | | For state purchase and control | 18.3% | | |
| | | | For national prohibition | 13.3% | | |
| 25 November 1972 | Multi-option poll | Alcohol licensing | For national continuance | 67.5% | 87.9% | Licensing Amendment Act 1910; Licensing Amendment Act 1918 |
| | | | For state purchase and control | 17.7% | | |
| | | | For national prohibition | 14.8% | | |
| 29 November 1975 | Multi-option poll | Alcohol licensing | For national continuance | 69.2% | 81.6% | Licensing Amendment Act 1910; Licensing Amendment Act 1918 |
| | | | For state purchase and control | 14.9% | | |
| | | | For national prohibition | 15.9% | | |

| Date | Poll type | Topic | Option | % | | Act |
|---|---|---|---|---|---|---|
| 25 November 1978 | Multi-option poll | Alcohol licensing | For national continuance<br>For state purchase and control<br>For national prohibition | 62.8%<br>15%<br>22.2% | 67.8% | Licensing Amendment Act 1910; Licensing Amendment Act 1918 |
| 28 November 1981 | Multi-option poll | Alcohol licensing | For national continuance<br>For state purchase and control<br>For national prohibition | 64%<br>14.1%<br>21.9% | 86.3% | Licensing Amendment Act 1910; Licensing Amendment Act 1918 |
| 14 July 1984 | Multi-option poll | Alcohol licensing | For national continuance<br>For state purchase and control<br>For national prohibition | 69.7%<br>11.7%<br>18.6% | 89.9% | Licensing Amendment Act 1910; Licensing Amendment Act 1918 |
| 15 August 1987 | Multi-option poll | Alcohol licensing | For national continuance<br>For state purchase and control<br>For national prohibition | 67.3%<br>12%<br>20.7% | 85.3% | Licensing Amendment Act 1910; Licensing Amendment Act 1918 |

a These votes were on a licencing district basis, however the results recorded in this schedule show the results on a national basis. Some districts did vote to restrict licencing (becoming "dry" districts), however the proportion of New Zealanders living in dry districts was never more than 16% (see Dostie and Dupré at 11).

b Voters could vote for one or two (but not three) of the available options).

c Voters could vote for one or two (but not three) of the available options).

d Voters could vote for one or two (but not three) of the available options).

e Voters could vote for one or two (but not three) of the available options).

f Voters could vote for one or two (but not three) of the available options).

g Amended the Licensing Act 1908 to establish national prohibition poll.

h Although more than 50% voted in favour of prohibition, the threshold for implementation was 60%. This was subsequently reduced to 50% in 1919.

i Amended the Licensing Act 1908 to require a further poll before 30 April 1919.

j Amended the Licensing Act 1908 to include option of state purchase and control.

### Local restoration polls 1996–1999: A note

"Local option" polls on alcohol licencing conditions were held from the late 19th and throughout the 20th century, supplementing the national alcohol licencing polls from 1911. The options were characterised as "wet" where alcohol sales were permitted, and "dry" where they were not. After 1918, local "wet" districts could no longer vote to go "dry" but "dry" districts were given the option of voting for the restoration of local licencing or to maintain their status. The supermajority requirement of 60% was also abolished in favour of a simple majority. Local alcohol licencing polls continued in the late 20th century (after the discontinuance of national prohibition polls) as the remaining "dry" districts voted on whether to end bans on alcohol licences.

The 1996 poll was held in four "dry" areas to coincide with the 1996 general election. Polls were held in Eden, Grey Lynn, Roskill, and Tawa. Turnout was 66,132 across the four districts. Local restoration received a majority in Grey Lynn (53% voting for restoration), however it was defeated on average across the four districts. A further poll was held in 1999 in the remaining dry districts: Eden, Roskill, and Tawa. A total of 53,445 voters participated and voted by 52.7% for local restoration in all three districts.

| Date | Form | Subject | Question | Votes in favour | Turnout of Electorate | Mechanism |
|---|---|---|---|---|---|---|
| 12 October 1996 | Single question | Liquor licenses in local districts | I vote for local restoration | 45.5% | N/A | Licensing Amendment Act 1910; Local Restoration Polls Act 1990 |
| | | | I vote for local no-licence | 54.5% | | |
| 27 November 1999 | Single question | Liquor licenses in local districts | I vote for local restoration | 52.7% | N/A | Licensing Amendment Act 1910; Local Restoration Polls Act 1990 |
| | | | I vote for local no-licence | 47.3% | | |

# Appendix III

## *Citizens Initiated Referenda Act Referendums 1993–2023*

| Date | Subject | Question | Votes in favour | Turnout of Electorate | Mechanism |
|---|---|---|---|---|---|
| 2 December 1995 | Reduction of number of professional fighters | Should the number of professional firefighters employed full time in the New Zealand Fire Service be reduced below the number employed on 1 January 1995? | 12.2% | 27.0% | Citizens Initiated Referenda Act 1993 |
| 27 November 1999 | Reform of the criminal justice system | Should there be a reform of our justice system placing greater emphasis on the needs of victims, providing restitution and compensation for them, and imposing minimum sentences and hard labour for all serious violent offences? | 91.75% | 82.9%[a] | Citizens Initiated Referenda Act 1993 |
| 27 November 1999 | Reduction of the number of MPs | Should the size of the House of Representatives be reduced from 120 members to 99 members? | 86.7% | 82.9%[b] | Citizens Initiated Referenda Act 1993 |
| 21 August 2008 | Should smacking be a criminal offence? | Should a smack as part of good parental correction be a criminal offence in New Zealand? | 12.0% | 56.1% | Citizens Initiated Referenda Act 1993; Referenda (Postal Voting) Act 2000 |
| 17 December 2012 | Privatisation of state-owned assets | Do you support the Government selling up to 49% of Meridian Energy, Mighty River Power, Genesis Power, Solid Energy and Air New Zealand? | 32.4% | 45.07% | Citizens Initiated Referenda Act 1993; Referenda (Postal Voting) Act 2000 |

[a] Held concurrently with the 1999 general election.
[b] Held concurrently with the 1999 general election.

*Appendices I–III compiled from:*

Nohlen, D., Hartmann, C. and Grotz, F. (2004). *Elections in Asia and the Pacific: a data handbook. Vol. II, South East Asia, East Asia and the South Pacific.* Oxford: Oxford University Press.

Stats NZ. *Yearbook collection: 1893–2012.* Available at: https://www.stats .govt.nz/indicators-and-snapshots/digitised-collections/yearbook-collec-tion-18932012/. (Accessed: 25 October 2023).

Wilson, J. O. (1985). *New Zealand Parliamentary Record: 1840-1984.* Wellington: Government Printer.

## Appendix IV

*New Zealand referendum legislation and ballot forms*

**1. Schedule 2 Electoral Referendum Act 2010 (enabling legislation for 2011 referendum)**

1 **Purpose of schedule**

The purpose of this schedule is to provide an outline of the key features of the voting systems that are options in the referendum. If the majority of votes in relation to Part A of the referendum voting paper support change to another voting system, further work will be needed to develop the details of the preferred voting system indicated by votes in relation to Part B of the referendum voting paper.

2 **Assumptions common to alternative voting systems**

(1) Parliament has 120 members.

(2) The principles for determining the number of members of Parliament who represent Māori electorates will not change.

(3) The principle of a fixed number of general electorate seats for the South Island will not change.

3 **Mixed member proportional representation voting system (MMP)**

(1) Parliament is made up of members who are elected by their respective electorates and members elected from party lists.

(2) Each voter has 2 votes

(a) a vote for a party; and

(b) a vote for his or her preferred candidate in his or her electorate.

(3) Each electorate elects 1 Member of Parliament on a First-Past-the-Post basis.

(4) The party vote is counted on a nationwide basis.

(5) A party may be eligible for a share of the list seats if the party gains 5% or more of the party vote or wins 1 or more electorate seats.

(6) The list seats in Parliament are allocated so that the total number of seats a party holds is in proportion to the number of party votes the party received, taking into account the number of electorate seats the party holds.

(7) A party's list seats are allocated to its candidates in the order in which they appear on the party's list (excluding those who win an electorate seat).

(8) A party may win a greater number of electorate seats than the number of seats to which it would be entitled by reason of the party vote result. In that case, the party keeps the electorate seats. In order to maintain proportionality, the number of list seats in Parliament increases by the difference for that term of Parliament. The extra seats are commonly known as the overhang.

## 4 First-past-the-post voting system (FPP)

(1) Parliament is made up of members who are elected by their respective electorates. There are no list members.

(2) Each voter has 1 vote.

(3) Each electorate elects 1 Member of Parliament.

(4) The winning candidate in each electorate is the one who gains the most votes.

## 5 Preferential voting system (PV)

(1) Parliament is made up of members who are elected by their respective electorates, and has no list members.

(2) Each electorate elects 1 member of Parliament.

(3) Voters rank the candidates in their electorate in order of preference by, for example, marking candidates 1, 2, 3, and so on.

(4) To win, a candidate must have 50% of the total votes cast plus 1 vote.

(5) The candidate with the most first-preference votes might not have more than 50% of the total votes cast. In that case, the votes for the candidate with the lowest number of first- preference votes are redistributed according to the second preferences of the voters for that candidate. Redistribution of preferences continues until a candidate attains more than 50% of the total votes cast.

## 6 Single transferable vote system (STV)

(1) Parliament is made up of members who are elected by their respective electorates, and has no list members.

(2) Each electorate elects several members of Parliament.

(3) Voters rank the candidates in their electorates in order of preference, for example 1, 2, 3, and so on. Alternatively, voters may vote for the order of preference decided in advance by a political party.

(4)  To win, a candidate must receive a minimum number of votes. The minimum number of votes is determined by a formula based on the number of seats allocated to the electorate.

(5)  Any candidate who receives more than the minimum number of first-preference votes is elected. If vacancies remain, the first-preference votes received by the elected candidates that are above the minimum required for their election are redistributed according to the second preferences. The redistribution starts with the largest surplus of votes.

(6)  If there are still vacancies after the distribution of surplus first-preference votes, the lowest- polling candidate is eliminated and all that candidate's votes are redistributed in line with the voters' second preferences, and so on. Any surplus votes from an elected candidate that were transferred to the lowest-polling candidate are redistributed in line with voters' third preferences.

(7)  If no candidate receives the minimum number of first-preference votes, the lowest-polling candidate is eliminated and all that candidate's votes are redistributed in line with the second preferences of the voters, and so on.

## 7    Supplementary member voting system (SM)

(1)  Parliament is made up of members who are elected by their respective electorates (they win **electorate seats**) and members returned from party lists (they win **supplementary seats**).

(2)  Of the 120 seats in Parliament, 90 would be electorate seats and 30 would be supplementary seats.

(3)  Each electorate elects 1 member of Parliament on a First-Past-the-Post basis.

(4)  Each voter has 2 votes

(a)  a vote for a party; and

(b)  a vote for his or her preferred candidate in his or her electorate.

(5)  The supplementary seats are allocated to parties in proportion to the number of party votes received by that party.

(6)  A party's supplementary seats are allocated to its candidates in the order in which they appear on the party's list, excluding those who win an electorate seat.

(7)  Only the supplementary seats are allocated in proportion to the number of votes received by a party's candidates or to the party vote. A party's share of supplementary seats is not affected by the number of electorate seats.

**2. Example of a first-stage "gateway and filter" ballot paper using First-Past-the-Post voting:**

**Ballot paper for the 2011 Electoral Referendum**

---

*[INSERT ELECTORATE NAME AND NUMBER]*                    *[Consecutive Number]*

## Referendum on New Zealand's Voting System

*[INSERT ELECTORATE NAME AND NUMBER]*

*Official Mart*

### Explanation

1. You may vote in **both Part A and Part B** or you may vote in **only Part A** or **only Part B**.
2. Vote by putting a tick in the circle next to the option you choose.

#### Part A

Should New Zealand keep the Mixed Member Proportional (MMP) voting system?

Vote Here

**Vote for only one option**

| I vote to **keep** the MMP voting system | ○ |
| I vote to **change** to another voting system | ○ |

#### Part B

If New Zealand were to change to another voting system, which voting system would you choose?

Vote Here

**Vote for only one option**

| I would choose the **First Past the Post** system (**FPP**) | ○ |
| I would choose the **Preferential Voting** system (**PV**) | ○ |
| I would choose the **Single Transferable Vote** system (**STV**) | ○ |
| I would choose the **Supplementary Member** system (**SM**) | ○ |

### Final Directions

- If you spoil this voting paper, return it to the officer who issued it and apply for a new paper.
- After voting, fold this voting paper so that its contents cannot be seen and **place it in the referendum ballot box.**
- You must not take this voting paper out of the polling place.

**3. Example of a first-stage "gateway and filter" referendum ballot paper using preferential voting:**

**Flag referendum 2015**

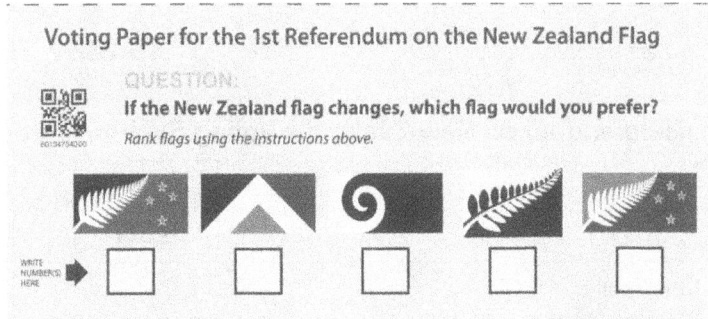

**4. Example of a second-stage "run-off" referendum ballot paper using First-Past-the-Post:**

**Flag referendum 2016**

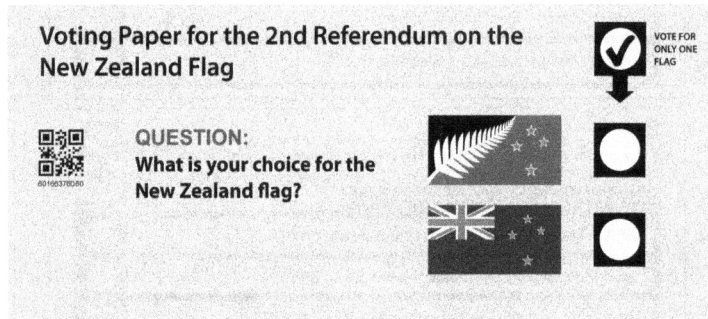

**5. Examples of legislative veto referendum ballot papers:**

(a) Electoral Reform referendum 1993
(b) End of Life Choice Act referendum 2020
(c) Cannabis Legislation and Control Bill referendum 2020

Vote Here

I vote for the present FIRST-PAST-THE-POST SYSTEM as provided in the Electoral Act 1956

I vote for the proposed MIXED MEMBER PROPORTIONAL SYSTEM as provided in the Electoral Act 1993

TICK ONE PROPOSAL

# REFERENDUMS VOTING PAPER

Official Mark

For each of the questions below, vote by putting a ✔ in the circle next to the option you choose.

## REFERENDUM 1: End of Life Choice Referendum

Do you support the End of Life Choice Act 2019 coming into force?

Vote for only one option

**Yes,** I support the End of Life Choice Act 2019 coming into force.

**No,** I do not support the End of Life Choice Act 2019 coming into force.

## REFERENDUM 2: Cannabis Referendum

Do you support the proposed Cannabis Legalisation and Control Bill?

Vote for only one option

**Yes,** I support the proposed Cannabis Legalisation and Control Bill.

**No,** I do not support the proposed Cannabis Legalisation and Control Bill.

**FINAL DIRECTIONS**
- If you spoill this voting paper, return it to the officer who issued it and apply for a new paper.
- After voting, fold this voting paper so that its contents cannot be seen and place it in the purple referendum ballot box
- You must not take this voting paper out of the voting place.

# Index

repeal of Crimes Act 17
representative democracy 2, 46
road maintenance 24
Robertson, John 36–37
Robertson, Margaret 22, 40
Royal Commission on the Electoral
    System (RCES) 16

sale of alcohol 12; *see also* alcohol
Sale of Liquor Act 1989 13
Schedule 2 Electoral Referendum
    Act 2010 (enabling legislation
    for 2011 referendum) 62–64
Seales, Lecretia 22, 26
second-stage run-off referendum
    ballot paper using First-Past-the-
    Post 66
Seddon, Richard 12, 25–26
self-determination referendums 7
single-option referendums,
    government-initiated
    referendums 14–15
single transferable vote system
    (STV) 63–64
size, of House of Representatives 17
size, of state: perceptual size 4;
    population measures 4; relational
    size 4
SM *see* supplementary member
    voting system
Social Credit Party 20

social movements 46
Stout, Robert 26
STV *see* single transferable
    vote system
superannuation referendum 23
supplementary member voting
    system (SM) 64

television 36
temperance movement 15
terms of parliament 14, 16, 29–30,
    36, 38, **51**
timing of referendums 29–31
Treaty of Waitangi 11, 23, 39
triennial liquor referendums 31–32, 38
trust in politicians 20
turnout for referendums 29–30

United Future Party 24

Victims' Rights Bill (2002) 40
voting reform 16, **51**; *see also*
    electoral reform

Ward, Joseph 12
wild pest control referendum
    petition 17
Withers, Norm 22

Young Greens 24

For Product Safety Concerns and Information please contact our EU
representative  GPSR@taylorandfrancis.com
Taylor & Francis Verlag GmbH, Kaufingerstraße 24, 80331 München, Germany

www.ingramcontent.com/pod-product-compliance
Lightning Source LLC
Chambersburg PA
CBHW061838220326
41599CB00027B/5330